THE CHÂTEAUX
OF GREATER PARIS

Text by
JANINE ET PIERRE SOISSON
Translated by David MaCrae

MINERVA

Flyleaf: The incomparable ornamental pond, by Latone, in front of the château of Versailles.
Page 1: Versailles: detail of the main façade.

Designed and Produced by
Editions Minerva SA, Genève

© Editions Minerva SA, Genève, 1983

Printed in Italy

THE CHÂTEAUX OF GREATER PARIS

Several rivers, principally the Aisne, Marne, Yonne and Eure, but also the Epte, Orne, Ourcq and others, flow into the Paris basin, which forms a ring around the city. It was for this reason that it was given the apt name of Ile-de-France in the 4th century.

The basin, which is geographically regular, is made up of tertiary deposits with broad alluvial plateaux and hills covered with a wide variety of forests. The area is divided into eleven regions, or *pays,* each with its characteristics; they include the Pays de France, le Parisis, le Beauvaisis, le Vexin, etc.

Paris, at the heart of Ile-de-France, gets its name from that of an ancient tribe called the Parisis, which established itself on an island in the Seine in the 3rd century BC. This settlement was later to become the Ile de la Cité. In 52 BC the Gauls, under their chief Camulogenus, were defeated by Julius Caesar's lieutenant Labienus. The straggling settlement was renamed Lutetia and became transformed into a real Gallo-Roman town, with an amphitheater, thermal baths, a

forum and an aqueduct. The town was later fortified against the Germans and within its walls Julian, wrongly called the Apostate by the Christians, was proclaimed emperor by his forces. Julian was the first person to care passionately about Paris, as can be seen from his letters. The fortunes of the town were varied: as it grew it was attacked by the Barbarians, and after being saved by St. Geneviève, became the Christian capital of the Franks, through the influence of Clovis.

Later Paris had to be defended against the Norsemen under Eudes, *dux francorum,* who later became tutor to Charles III (the Simple) and even, for a time, the elected King of the Franks. In 893 he was to have shared his ex-pupil's crown and recognition as his successor, but never actually did so.

Louis V (known as *le Fainéant,* "the good-for-nothing"), who died without issue, was the last of the Carolingians; the crown then went to a great-nephew of Eudes, Hugues Capet, so named because of the cape which he always wore. The Capetians reigned until 1848 and because of them the history of France was centered on Paris. It was the focal point of attraction as much for the

richness of its agriculture as for its accessibility, by road and river, to all surrounding regions.

Gothic art was born in Ile-de-France, in the form of cathedrals, churches, monasteries and abbeys. The Renaissance may have given the Loire Valley many fine châteaux, but it was in Ile-de-France that the three styles which Louis XIV, Louis XV and Louis XVI produced left the best results of their influence. It was in this blessed region that landscape-gardening reached its highest point, evolving from the 16th-century garden, which was simply attached to the château, to the formal 17th-century garden and the superbly landscaped layouts of the 18th century.

We hope that we can tempt readers of this book to join in on an imaginary visit to this region which is the very heart of France.

Left: The golden door of the château of Fontainebleau. Above: The château of Maintenon, with its square turret contrasting with the round towers.

3

THE LOUVRE

The Louvre is one of the greatest monuments in France, and is the biggest of the palaces of the French kings. The origin of its name is obscure; it could come from the Latin word for wolf *(lupus)*, or from the old Saxon word *lower,* meaning 'fortified habitation'. We know that it was called the Louvre in 1190 when King Philippe-Auguste decided to build a rampart and fortress along the Seine against the ever-present danger of flooding. Construction was finished in 1202. This was the start of an architectural development which was to involve the most powerful kings, two emperors and three republics.

Some outlines on the ground are all that remains of Philippe-Auguste's keep and its rectangular precincts. It was never inhabited but was used to house the crown treasures, weapons and some prisoners. Louis IX *(le Saint)* had a chapel and a huge hall added; in the 14th century Charles V decided to live there and converted it

into a residence. The walls of Paris were lengthened and the Louvre no longer had an exclusively military role. The king was given his pseudonym *le Sage,* "the Wise", when he installed his famous library in one of the towers. The 973 manuscripts in the library were considered to be a huge collection at the time. Then, for 150 years, the Louvre was quiet and almost abandoned, because Charles VI and his successors preferred to live in Paris mansions such as the Hôtel St. Pol and the Tournelles. In their youth they spent much of their time at their châteaux on the Loire.

François I wanted to show his gratitude to the citizens of Paris for contributing a large part of his ransom after the disastrous defeat at Pavia. He settled in the capital and had the grim old keep demolished. He had the architect Pierre Lescot and the sculptor Jean Goujon build a palace. François died having seen only the foundations completed, but his son Henri II carried on with the work and added another wing. His three grandsons François II, Charles IX and Henri III, and their successor Henri IV, each took over

responsibility for the work. Pierre Lescot died in 1571 while it was still in progress.

Sumptuous feasts were held in the famous Salle des Cariatides, including the wedding banquets of the future King François II and of the future King Henri and Queen Margot. Coligny was killed by a shot from an arquebus as he left the Louvre, forty-eight hours after the Saint Bartholomew's Day Massacre. It was in Queen Margot's bedroom at the Louvre that, during that same bloody night, a wounded Huguenot hid from the crazed

mob. "The man threw himself on my bed to save himself. I felt that I was being held by a man and threw myself into the space between the bed and the wall. He fell after me and we both screamed at the same time, each as scared as the other. Finally, thanks be to God, Monsieur de Nancais, the captain of the guards, found me in this terrible state. Although he was visibly worried, he couldn't help laughing."

In 1585, in the Salle des Cariatides, Henri III had 120 page boys "with handkerchiefs over their faces, with holes at the eyes" beaten for insolently imitating the king and his minions in a penitents' procession. It was there also that a terrible scene took place with his sister Margot, in which he treated her like a prostitute, enumerating her many lovers. Here, during the League, the duc de Mayenne hanged four leaders of the Conseil des Seize from the beams, and here also the people filed past the remains of good King Henri IV—or a model representing him— after his assassination by Ravaillac, Louis XIV washed the feet of thirty poor people here every Maundy Thursday and Molière performed before the king for the first time on May 4 1658. The program consisted of *Nicomède* and *Le Dépit amoureux*.

The most spacious monument in Paris and the first palace of the kings of France — The Louvre.

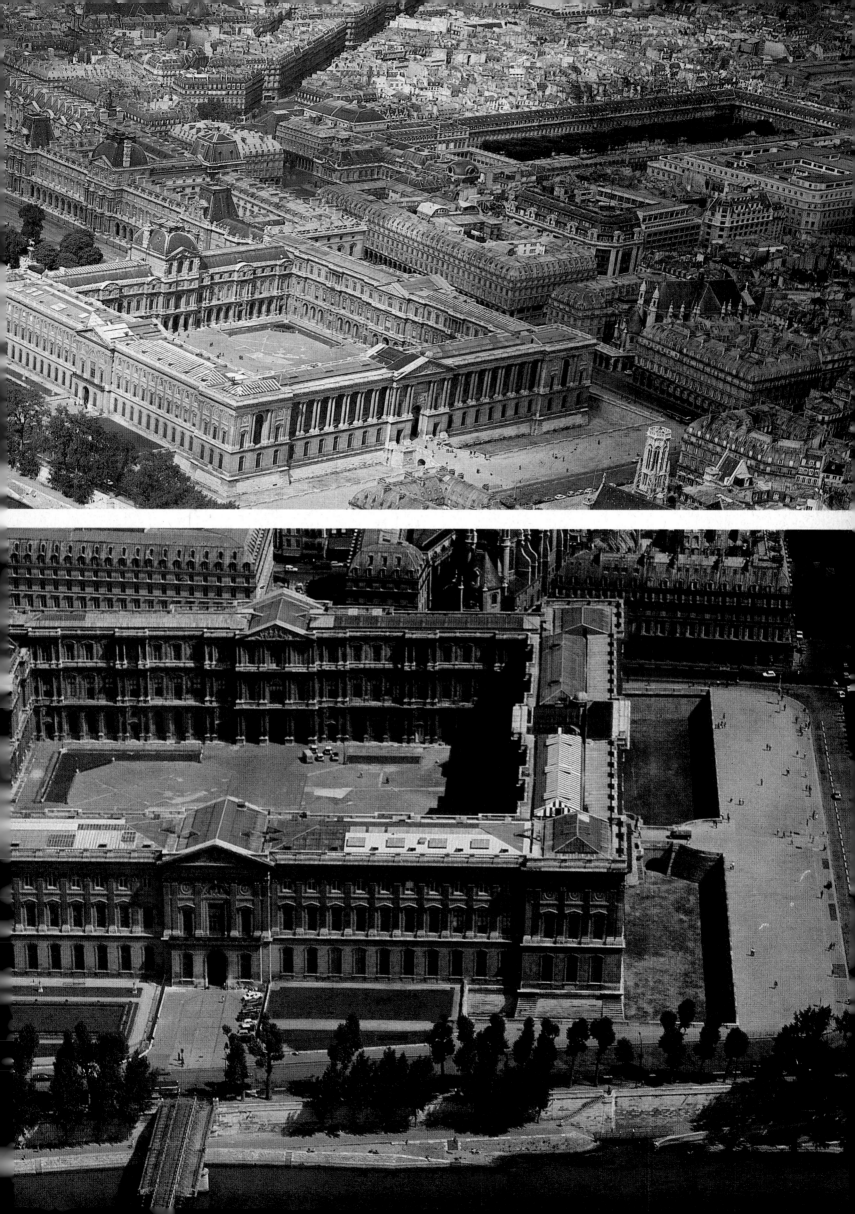

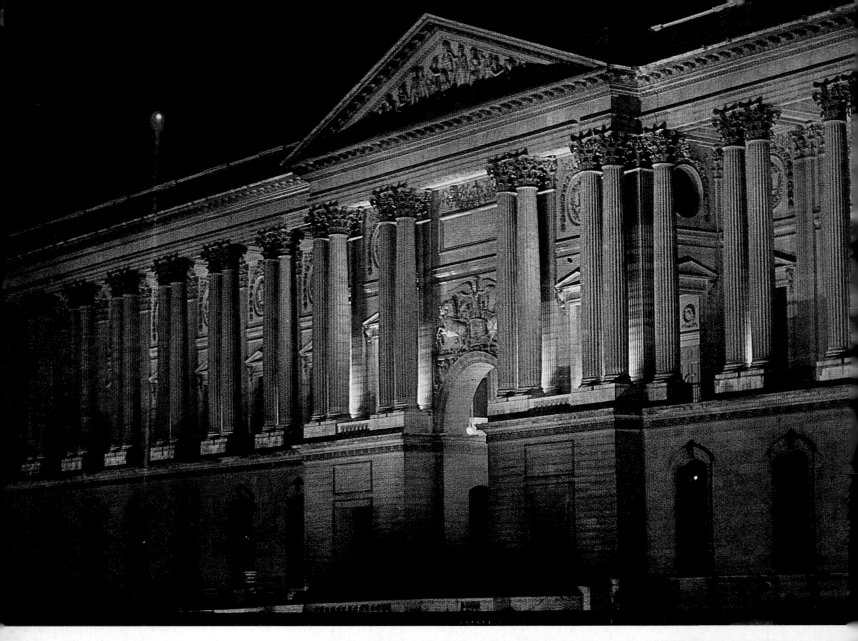

The Royal Apartments, most notably those of the Queen Mother, are in the south wing of the Old Louvre. Catherine de Médicis, Marie de Médicis and Ann of Austria all lived there, the latter also dying there, of breast cancer. Legend has it that it was from a balcony in this apartment that Charles IX amused himself by shooting at Protestants during the Saint Bartholomew' Day Massacre. This story is actually untrue, because the balcony did not exist at the time.

Throughout this period construction proceeded relentlessly. In 1563 Catherine de Médicis decided to move out of the Hôtel des Tournelles, where her husband had died so tragically. She gave orders that a place should be built not far from the Louvre, the future Tuileries, and for two connecting galleries to be built between them. The Tuileries was abandoned soon after its construction—being too close to Saint-Germain-l'Auxerrois— when the queen was told of a prediction to the effect that she would die "near Saint-Germain". In actual fact Catherine may as well have stayed where she was, since she was attended, in her dying moments at Blois, by none other than Monseigneur... de Saint-Germain!

Preceding pages: Two general views of the Louvre. The Louvre: The façade and a detail of the Cour Carrée (Square Courtyard).

Boudin, a former policeman who had been dismissed, "Colonel" Blériot, an ex-butcher, and "General" Bergeret, a printer. The fire sped through the Louvre's attics in no time. The art treasures were saved through the courage of the curator, Barbet de Jouy, and a young craftsman, Héron de Ville-Forse, who, helped by a few attendants, beat the worst of the blaze before the 26th battalion of Chasseurs arrived. The fire destroyed the Pavillon de Marzan, the Tuileries, the west half of the Napoleon wing and the hundred thousand books stored in the perpendicular wing.

The remains of the Palais des Tuileries were razed to the ground. Lefuel rebuilt the burnt-out parts of the Louvre between 1873 and 1875. In 1876 the Ministry of Finance moved in.

The idea of establishing the Louvre as a museum occurred to the marquis de Marigny after the success of an exhibition of painting of King Louis XV in the Luxembourg.

The government collapsed, but this did not affect either the plans, or the law of May 6 1791 which established the Louvre as a Museum of the Arts of the Republic. The museum was opened on August 10 1793. It was the pinnacle of achievement for this huge building, filled with history and universally famous. But that is another story.

Below: The Arc de Triomphe of the Carrousel in the heart of the palace gardens.

Henri IV more or less finished the two galleries and also added another floor and the Pavillon de Flore. The galleries accommodated a number of shops which were later to be used exclusively by artists. Louis XIII decided that the Louvre was too small, and set about quadrupling its size. The tower containing Charles V's library was demolished. Le Mercier followed Lescot's style when he built the three-story Pavillon Sully and lengthened it with a group of symmetrical buildings. A fourth floor held four groups of two cariatids, the work of Sarrazin.

After the Fronde, Louis XIV decided to live in the Louvre, because he felt more secure than in the Palais-Royal. He had some extravagant plans for the place, and had what was left of the original buildings pulled down, as well as enclosing the town houses and other structures situated between the wings. Bernini arrived on the scene, having been summoned from Italy, with bold plans to raze almost everything. Louis XIV preferred the plans of Claude Perrault, Le Brun and Le Van for the Colonnade.

In 1668 the Sun-King gave orders for the wing bordering on the Seine to be expanded, but construction stopped when he changed his mind, deciding to live at Versailles instead. For the second time, the Louvre was abandoned by the Court. For 120 years it was subjected to a variety of indignities: houses were built in the interior, and wine-shops and cheap restaurants were set up. Right next to the Academies of the Sciences, Fine Arts, Painting and Sculpture there came into being a whore-infested area of hovels and shanties.

In 1756, Madame de Pompadour's brother, Marigny, Superintendent of the King's Buildings, decided to expel all undesirable characters and to demolish the buildings in the courtyard in an effort to restore this dilapidated place to something of its past grandeur. Construction was held up, however, and the royal buildings were looted and ransacked during the Revolution. It was not until the First Empire that the Cour Carrée was completed and the north and south wings had a second floor added, to bring them up to the level of the west wing. The Colonnade was not finished until 1811, along with the Napoleon Gallery, which runs the length of the rue de Rivoli, and the Marsan and Rohan Pavilions. The latter was finished under Louis XIII, and it was Napoleon III who finally put the finishing touches to the "Grand Dessein".

Haussmann himself admitted that he had feathered his nest by demolishing all the houses in the Carrousel, an impressive courtyard so named because of the great festivals which used to be held there, including military parades, assorted games and theatrical productions. The Arc de Triomphe was commissioned by Napoleon I. Visconti and Lefuel built the two parallel buildings at each side of the Carrousel and joined them to the rue de Rivoli wing. Tall pavilions were built at the intersections and the existing façades were altered to give a more cohesive look to the entire place.

The fall of the Second Empire was a dangerous time for the Louvre. During the night of 23/24 May 1871, the Tuileries was set on fire by some "officers" of the Commune: "Capitaine"

THE LUXEMBOURG

Conseiller Alexandre de la Tourette built a private townhouse in 1564. It was constructed on a site formerly occupied by a Roman camp, near a Carthusian monastery. The Queen Regent Marie de Médicis bought the property from the duc de Luxembourg in 1612. The queen, tired of the Louvre, built a palace which would remind her of her native Italy. The architect Salomon de Bross was inspired by the Pitti Palace in Florence when he designed this well-constructed building which is symmetrically arranged around a central court-yard opening out throught a triumphal entrance topped with a dome.

In the 19th century Alphonse de Gisors enlarged it in the style of the original, adding an avantcorps and galleries in the garden which formed a new façade. The magnificent formal gardens were expanded over the centuries, to the detriment of the Carthusian monastery and its nursery. The famous Médicis Fountain, the work of Nicolas de Brosses, was constructed in 1620 and moved in 1860.

The queen did not enjoy living in her palace, which had been richly decorated by Rubens, for very long. She settled there in 1625 and promptly began plotting against Cardinal de Richelieu– unwisely, as it turned out, since by November 11 1630, after a short-lived triumph known as the "Journée des Dupes", she found herself defeated by the cardinal. Marie went into exile and died in wretched circumstances in Cologne.

A Parisian poet, Claude Le Petit, recorded her end in the following leaden verse:

Quand j'admire solidement
Cet admirable bâtiment
Qui semble au Louvre faire niche,
Je dis : Est-ce possible enfin

Que celle qui l'a fait si riche
Soit morte à Cologne de faim ?

The palace passed to Gaston d'Orléans, then to his daughter, La Grande Demoiselle.

During the Terror it was converted into a prison called the "Maison Nationale de Sûreté". The first people to make use of it were the Girondins, before going to the guillotine, the

The Luxembourg Palace and its famous gardens, offering delightful walks to countless visitors. Below: The Médicis Fountain, to the left of the palace.

dreaded Hébert and his compatriots, followed by Danton, Camille and Lucile Le Desmoulins, Fabre d'Églantine, author of *Il pleut bergère* and the republican calendar. Another man who spent time there was the mountain-dwelling painter David.

In 1795 the Directoire moved into the palace, and in 1800 it was earmarked for the Senate. The Restoration saw it being used for the Chambre des Pairs. Marshal Ney was tried there, as was Louis Napoléon Bonaparte after his landing at Boulogne. Louis made the Luxembourg Palace the home of the Senate, which it still is today.

THE CONCIERGERIE

The Palais de Justice, incorporating the Sainte-Chapelle and the Conciergerie, stands opposite Notre-Dame on the outskirts of the Ile-de-la-Cité. The Merovingian and Carolingian kings lived in the Conciergerie, the medieval section of which is built on the site of the 4th-century Roman governors' residence. Louis VI and Louis VII lived and died there. Philippe Auguste was born there, and Saint Louis, who built the Sainte-Chapelle, lived there also. Philippe the Fair ordered Enguerrand de Marigny to enlarge the old palace with the addition of the Tour d'Argent, the Tour César and three magnificent Gothic halls. In the 19th century the whole palace was restored by Viollet-le-Duc.

The name of the Conciergerie derives from the high office of the Concierge, a kind of powerful Superintendent and Provost. As it was his job to administer justice, he converted a tower in the palace into a prison. It later came to be called the Montgomery Tower, in memory of the unfortunate knight who killed Henri II in a tournament, and was imprisoned there some years later. In those days the Tour d'Argent and the Tour César were called the Tournelle Criminelle and the Tournelle Civile, being used as meeting-places for legal counsel on criminal and civil cases respectively. In the oldest of the towers, the Tour Bonbec, prisoners were tortured in order to loosen their tongues—whence the name, from *bec,* "mouth" or "beak".

In 1481 the Conciergerie was the site of the massacre of the Armagnacs. Later on the regicides Ravaillac, Damiens, Louvel and Fieschi were incarcerated there. The heyday of the Conciergerie was the Revolution. Queen Marie-Antoinette spent the last days of her life there, imprisoned with her sister-in-law Madame Elisabeth, Char-

lotte Corday, Madame du Barry, Lavoisier ("The Republic does not need scientists" said Fouquier-Tinville), and also André Chénier ("And it doesn't need poets, either!"). At one end of the guard room, behind a grill was the preserve of the executioner, Samson; he was known as Monsieur de Paris, from the name Rue de Paris. Many victims left the Conciergerie through the *Galerie des Prisonniers* and the *Cour du Mai* only to perish on the scaffold.

Left and above: The Conciergerie (prison). Marie-Antoinette, Charlotte Cordey and many others were imprisoned here during the Revolution. Right: The Tour de l'Horloge (Clock Tower) and the vaulting of the kitchens.

THE PALAIS-ROYAL

In 1624 Cardinal de Richelieu put Jacques Le Mercier in charge of building a distinctive residence opposite the Louvre on the site of several houses, one of which belonged to the marquise de Rambouillet, known also as La Divine Artémise. The classically styled cardinal's palace consisted of a main section with two wings, eight courtyards and a theater where Molière and Lulli performed. The present Théâtre de la Comédie-Française was built between 1787 and 1790. The cardinal bequeathed his residence to Louis XIII and it then became the Palais Royal. After his death Ann of Austria lived there with her two sons. It is said that the young King Louis XIV fell into the Grand Bassin while playing with young friends and narrowly escaped drowning. The royal family lived there during the terrible days of the Fronde. During the night of February 9-10 1651 the Parisian mob invaded the palace, demanding confirmation of the actual presence of the royal infant in his bedroom. It was an unprecedented humiliation.

Louis XIV was not particularly fond of the palace. He installed Madame Henriette, widow of Charles I of England, there and then gave it to the queen's daughter when she married Philippe d'Orléans, the king's brother.

On the sudden demise of this princess—immortalized by Bossuet, the great preacher, in a very famous and appreciated funeral oration—the palace passed into the Orléans family.

Under Louis XVI, the future Philippe Égalité turned a handsome profit by building on three sides of the garden and selling the property off as shops and apartments. It was a popular place where one could find elegant shops alongside gaming houses, disreputable dives and whorehouses.

It was here that Camille Desmoulins, bearing a badge featuring a chestnut tree leaf, incited the

crowds on the day before the storming of the Bastille.

The palace was to become the seat of the Tribunat, and later of the Tribunal de Commerce and the Bourse (stock exchange). It survived an attempt by the Commune to burn it down. Today it is home to the Conseil d'État, the Conseil Constitutionnel and several of the services of the Administration des Beaux-Arts. The garden is blissfully quiet. Cocteau lived and Colette died near this truly beautiful place.

Above and left: Different views of the Palais-Royal (Royal Palace) and its colonnades. Right (top): The west gallery of the building. (Bottom): The courtyard of the Bourbon Palace (where the National Assembly now meets).

THE PALAIS-BOURBON

Louise-Françoise de Bourbon, who was officially recognized as the daughter of Louis XIV and Madame de Montespan, commissioned Ghirardini to build the Palais-Bourbon in 1722. Construction started under Lassurance and was finished in 1728 by Gabriel and Aubert. Louis XIV bought it in order to incorporate it into the square which, in those days, bore his name—the modern Place de la Concorde. He then sold it to the prince de Condé. The prince carried out certain radical alterations, enlarging the building by adding two wings at each side of the *cour d'honneur* and rounding it off nicely with two columned pavilions.

The Palais-Bourbon was confiscated during the Revolution. In 1795 one section of it was used as the meeting place of the Conseil des Cinq-Cents. The École Polytechnique, which at that time was a

day school, used the premises, and archives were also stored there.

In 1806 Napoleon decided to complete the church of La Madeleine, where he wanted to create a "Temple of Glory". During the construction of this building the architect laid out the façade in portico form with twelve Corinthian columns. The pediment was carved by Cortot in 1841 and the two low-reliefs were the work of Rude and Pradier.

In 1815 the Palais-Bourbon was given back to the prince de Condé. The State bought part of it from his son in 1827 for 5.5 million francs, so that the representatives could continue to sit there. The July Monarchy acquired the rest for 5,047,475 francs, and since then the palace has always been used by government representatives.

ECOUEN

The construction of the château of Ecouen, which is both manor and citadel, was started by the rich constable Anne de Montmorency, the son of illustrious parents, a marshal, peer of the realm and childhood friend of François I. It took forty years to complete. Ecouen stayed in the family until 632, when the heir, Henri II, duc de Montmorency, was sentenced to death by the Parliament of Toulouse and beheaded for conspiring with Gaston d'Orléans against Louis XIII and Cardinal de Richelieu.

The château became the property of the duchesse d'Angoulême and then of the Condé family, in which it stayed until the Revolution, when it was confiscated under the laws concerning property. Napoleon saved it from ruin by using it to house a school for the daughters of members of the Legion of Honor, under Madame Campan, the former chambermaid of Marie-Antoinette. In 1814 it was returned to its rightful owners, the Condé family, but it reverted to the State in 1830. The very interesting Musee National de la Renaissance has been housed in it since 1962.

The architecture of Ecouen, which has been attributed to Jean Bullant, though Jean Goujon also worked on it, represents one of the first samples in France of the "colossal order" which marked the transition from the first Renaissance period —that of the châteaux of the Loire— to the Henri II, or second Renaissance style.

Above: Two views of the château of Écouen, which houses the National Renaissance Museum. Below: A red marble fireplace and Psyche's Gallery. Right (bottom): Meudon Observatory, on the site of the old château.

MEUDON

The woods of Meudon, in which Parisians love to stroll on Sundays, are situated on a plateau overlooking the Seine Valley, with a total surface area of nearly three thousand acres.

In the 16th century the duchesse d'Etampes and then Cardinal Charles de Lorraine had huge gardens laid out at the edge of this forest, around a château near where the modern observatory is located. This old château was demolished in 1804, though its splendid terrace, which still remains, provides an extraordinary view of one of the finest landscapes near Paris.

The new château, now occupied by the observatory, was built by Mansart in 1706 for the Grand Dauphin, the son of Louis XIV. When he visited the building the Sun-King was not at all impressed. "Good Lord!" he said, "this looks more like the house of a rich financier than the abode of a great prince!" and turned on his heel without even crossing the threshhold, much to the amazement of his courtiers.

In 1870 the château was gutted by fire by the Prussians, but was later restored. This was done because, notwithstanding the great monarch's disdain, Meudon is a very pretty place, which is why it has always been a privileged place of residence.

Rabelais was the curate of this charming village. Ronsard lived there, as did Ambroise Paré and Armande Béjart, dame Molière, whose house was later turned into a museum. Wagner stayed some time at Meudon, and Rodin, whose property in the Val Fleuri still contains some of his wonderful work, was also a resident.

In the garden the very famous statue of *The Thinker* tower over his tomb in profound meditation.

VERSAILLES

At the beginning of the 17th century, Versailles was a very plain little village next to a knoll on which there stood a farmhouse—doubtless the last vestige of feudal times. All around were marsh lands, thickets and forest. Louis XIII was specially fond of this area because of the abundance of game, and he went hunting there frequently, both with coursing hounds and bow and arrow. In 1624 he bought some land and built a hunting lodge on it. Seven years later, Jean-Francois de Gondi, who had succeeded his brother Henri as bishop of Paris, ceded the Versailles estate to his sovereign. Philibert Le Roy then turned the royal lodge into a small château.

This elegant but modest building was to serve as the core of the gigantic château of Louis XIV, who constantly expanded and improved it throughout the last fifty years of his reign.

It is important to remember Louis XIV's childhood, which was disturbed by the civil strife connected with the Fronde. When the screaming mob swarmed into the Palais Royal demanding to see the king, who, they were quite sure, had been kidnapped by Mazarin and taken out of Paris, he was only twelve years old. Events left their imprint on him. He experienced the aristocratic insurrection known as the Fronde des Seigneurs, but also those of the Parliaments and of the people. Together, they made up a harsh lesson, which the adolescent Louis would never forget. Forever after he trusted nobody and nothing. He was particularly distrustful towards the riot-prone populace of Paris. His fears were based not only on his own personal experience but also on that of his ancestor, Charles V, who had been prevented from leaving the capital and who could merely watch powerlessly as his counsellors were massacred. He decided therefore that both he and his government would have their seat outside the city, in a royal town where popular commotion would not bother him. This was a wise precaution, which Louis XVI failed to take when, in October 1789, he agreed to return to Les Tuileries, with an escort 'of his good people'. Louis XIV decided that this royal and administrative town would be Versailles, a good distance from Paris, and a place where he had already hunted.

He foiled the Parliaments by the *lettre patente* of 1673, which compelled these assemblies to register edicts before presenting complaints, which were thenceforth without effect. He was also, and particularly, distrustful of the nobility; indeed throughout his life he worked hard to neutralize it and lower its standing. He attracted the great lords around him, turning them into the puppets of a sumptuous court, into manservants who, though covered with honors, were nonetheless under his heel. He also caused them to put severe strains on their finances: far away from home the nobles lived extravagantly, trying to outdo each other in elegance and lavishness, losing huge sums of money at the gaming tables and limiting their fighting spirit to the derisory quest for a royal smile. For this purpose, he needed not only an immense château - one which, in the middle of his reign, accomodated a thousand nobles and four thousand servants—but also a full-scale town to accomodate some ten thousand soldiers, five thousand servants and a host of people drawn there by the proximity of the court. This led Louis XIV to build a monumental château over five hundred yards long, and to lay out at its feet a town, whose broad and uncluttered streets were esthetically and strategically a complete success and in which he distributed plots of land to whomever he saw fit, in return for a tax of only five *sous* per *arpent* (acre). His zoning ordinances, however, were exceedingly strict: for example, the maximum height for any building was the level of the château courtyard! Versailles is thus the magnificent seat of a triumphant absolute monarchy.

Versailles: The main entrance, the courtyard and the wing called the Ministers' Wing. Right: Different details of the main gate, with its remarkable effigy of the Sun-King (top).

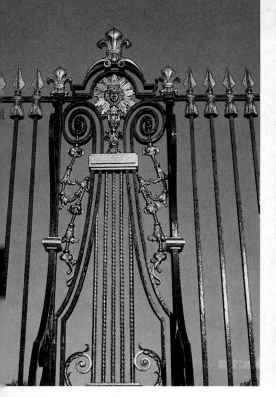

A TRULY HERCULEAN TASK

Upon the death of Mazarin, in 1661, the young king—who was not even twenty-five at the time—decided to reign alone. One of his richest and most powerful subjects, his financial superintendent, Nicolas Fouquet, made one fatal mistake: the festivities to which he had invited the monarch at his château of Vaux-le-Vicomte. In August 1661, proved to be so lavish that Louis XIV was profoundly ashamed and humiliated. Nicolas Fouquet was arrested nineteen days later and ended his days in prison. However, while the king was quite prepared to forget all about his former superintendent, languishing away in his jail, he never forgot the marvellous château of Vaux-le-Vicomte and its splendor. As a result he summoned all the artists who had worked on it and commissioned them to build his projected palace at Versailles. These included the architect Louis Le Vau, the landscape artist André Le Nôtre and the decorator Charles Le Brun. Le Vau died in 1670; his work was taken over by the thirty-year-old Jules Hardouin-Mansart, who devoted the rest of his life to the venture. The two Italian engineers, father and son, by the name of Francine, took charge of all the hydraulic engineering—not an easy or a modest undertaking, as there were 1,400 fountains at Versailles! They had to divert the Bièvre river, drain the nearby plateaux and then use the machine at Marly, built between 1681 and 1684, which drew water from the Seine to supply the rather large ponds at Versailles. Construction was even started on an aqueduct across the Maintenon Valley, from the Eure to Versailles. Malaria decimated the workers engaged in this project, and when the war came the structure was abandoned with just over half a mile of it complete.

All the construction at Versailles was on a Herculean scale—it lasted more than fifty years and kept thirty-six thousand workers busy. To begin with, they had to build a hill, as the original knoll was not large enough to support a château of the intended dimensions. So they went ahead and changed the face of the landscape. Around the hill thus formed a forest was planted, the marshes were drained dry, 250 acres of gardens were laid out, ponds and canals were dug—the Grand Canal is almost a mile long—, an Orangerie with three thousand shrubs was designed, with copses and a rock garden, and a hunting preserve of over 16,000 acres was enclosed. All of this was designed and realized by the extraordinary Le Nôtre, whose glory has, for three centuries, been unceasingly proclaimed "by these palaces of foliage which he designed and erected, and by those ponds where the water has slept silently for so long and to which his genius has miraculously given grace, suppleness, diversity and life".

Little by little the château rose from its foundations, spread, gained in height and also in length. The last building to be constructed during the reign of Louis XIV was the chapel, which was completed by Robert de Cotte in 1710.

The king was always present in these ambitious projects. He gave the first indications, made sure his wishes were met, corrected plans and worried about the finest details. He was in fact the prime architect and the great coordinator of this superb structure.

Versailles: Left: The Salon de la Paix (Hall of Peace) and the apartments of Louis XIV. Right: One of the numerous fireplaces and a view of the very famous Galerie des Glaces (Mirror Gallery). Following pages: General perspective of the Galerie des Glaces.

STONE AND GLORY

"In order to have Versailles the way it is today, Louis XIV had to resign himself to living among the dust of demolition, the mortar of masons and the nerve-shattering noise of stone-dressing... from 1665 to 1710! Forty-five years of scaffolding, ladders, gravel, earth-moving, marble-sawing, stone-hoisting, the rumble of wheelbarrows, of heavy carts stuck in the mud, of air filled with fine plaster. One would really have to be in love with building in order to endure such a life. And the miraculous thing is that it is so beautiful! It was gradually built up around the small château of Louis XIII which they did not even have time to demolish, and which disappeared, in the midst of such a grandiose structure like a truffle in a superb *pâté*." (G. Lenôtre)

The roofs of this three-storey palace are generally flat; those facing the garden are hidden behind a balustrade, while there are Mansart-style windows along the roofs looking over the courtyard. The Grandes and the Petites Ecuries (stables) are two symmetrical buildings, the work of Jules Hardouin-Mansart, which are aligned on the Avenue de Paris, in the town of Versailles. They could accomodate two thousand five hundred horses and were used for tournaments. In order to reach the château, which is separated from the stables by the parade ground, the visitor had to pass through immense wrought-iron gates and cross three courtyards: the forecourt, or Cour des Ministres, surrounded by buildings which served as accomodation for the members of the government and to which carriages were admitted; the Cour Royale, which in those days was closed off by a wrought-iron grill where the statue of Louis XIV now stands and which could be entered only by royal carriages; the Cour de Marbre, which stands at the top of several steps, was paved with black and white marble in those days and is surrounded on three sides by the original small château.

This latter was actually much renovated by Le Vau and Mansart. Under Louis XIV its

ground floor was used as a vestibule and provided access from the courtyard to the gardens. Louis XV later built his private quarters there. The Sun-King occupied the huge, sumptuous and highly decorative rooms, wholly lacking in cosi-

Versailles: Left: The golden gate of the Grand Trianon and the theater of the château; Above: Part of the main façade and the raised garden of the Grand Trianon.

ness, which look out over the marble courtyard, on the second floor. His bedroom is aligned along the axis of the château, facing the rising sun, as one might expect. The lavish ceremonies of the Royal Rising and Going to Bed took place in this room, which was also where the king breathed his last.

His apartments, drawing rooms, bathrooms and antechambers are on one side; those of the queen form a matching set. The Salon de l'Œil-de-Bœuf ("bull's-eye"), next to the royal bedroom, owes its name to a round opening above the fireplace and the pier; it was used as a waiting room for courtiers, who would crowd into it, hoping anxiously to be noticed by the sovereign.

Two reigns later, on October 6 1789, the rioters stopped just behind the leaves of the door to this drawing room. In the formal ceremonial bedroom of Louis XIV, vhich he no longer occupied, his descendant Louis XVI, fearing for his life, clutched his wife and his two children close to him. Through the window he looked out at the scene in the Cour Royale, into which the attackers were pouring, and he heard the insults shouted against the "slut" and the "woman from Austria". This was where the long sufferings of the royal family began.

Behind the queen's apartments three small and modest rooms accomodated Mme de Maintenon, the former Françoise d'Aubigné, also known as

Widow Scarron. Under her influence the court, which had become austere, would gather in these small rooms around its ageing sovereign and his morganatic wife to enjoy virtuous pleasures. In this intimate setting Racine read *Esther* and *Athalie*.

The façade facing the park, and particularly the famous Galerie des Glaces, were built by Le Vau and completed by Mansart in 1687. In this hall, the most beautiful in the most beautiful palace in the world, with a length of 246 feet, seventeen mirror panels face seventeen windows which are superbly exposed to the setting sun. It came into being almost as an afterthought, through a series of apartments which formed wings and which were separated, at the level of the second floor, by a broad balcony with a pool. Yet it has been an immense success, and in the best taste.

One wonders how many memories are reflected in these mirrors, which were cast in the recently established factory of the Faubourg Saint-Antoine! They have looked down on the great king, amorous and sprightly and later ageing and hardened, but never bowed by the years. How many queens and beautiful women have admired themselves in these mirrors! Madame de Pompadour may have gazed into them as she altered the position of a beauty spot at the corner of her lip; Madame Du Barry, nervous on the day of her presentation at court, could see the paleness of her skin through her make-up; Marie-Antoinette, the blonde and pink archduchess of sixteen may have grazed them with the tips of her slender fingers. These mirrors have seen pass before them Condé and Villars, and Jean Bart, pipe in mouth, then later on the ageing Franklin with his down-at-heel shoes.

The grandest celebrations took place here, in a setting of unheard-of luxury, before the throne, which was situated at one end of the hall, next to the Salon de la Paix. There are several other drawing rooms surrounding the Galerie des Glaces, each of them being designated in accordance with its decor. Buffet and gaming tables were set up, as well as platforms for orchestras; these rooms were illuminated by hundreds of chandeliers, girandoles and candelabras, while the guests danced in formal court dress covered with satin, silk and precious stones.

It was in the same Galerie des Glaces that Otto von Bismarck, the Iron Chancellor, in the presence of Wilhelm I, proclaimed the German Empire, on January 18 1871. On June 26 1919, the Treaty of Versailles and the Covenant of the

Versailles: Various views of the most beautiful park in the world.

League of Nations were signed in this same room.

The decor is incredibly luxurious: there are countless painted panels, the finest of which are the work of Le Brun, large areas of gilt, sculptures, colored marbles, statues in the ancient style, coffered ceilings, inlaid wood floors, iridescent tapestries from the Gobelins Royal Factory, and from the Savonnerie Carpet Works, as well as carved bronzes and copper, each item seeking to outdo the others in beauty and richness.

Two wings extend the château in opposite directions: the north wing contains the chapel and ends at the opera house. This theater, unusual at the time on account of its oval shape, was built by Gabriel in 1768, at the end of the reign of Louis XV. It was inaugurated for the celebrations of the wedding of his grandson, the Dauphin, later Louis XVI, and Archduchess Marie-Antoinette. It is remarkable for both its decor and its acoustics.

On the other side of the main part of the château is the matching south wing, which extends behind the triple arcade of the Cour des Princes. This was where the Enfants de France (Princes and Princesses of the blood) used to live, together with the members of the royal family.

THE TRIANONS

Just over half a mile from the Bassin de Neptune Louis XIV built a fragile château whose outer and inner surfaces were both clad in Delft ceramic tiles; it was named Le Trianon de Porcelaine and provided the king with a place where he could meet Madame de Montespan. The deterioration of the ceramics followed the favorite royal mistress's fall from favor, in connection with the "Affair of the Poisons". In less than a year Louis XIV built a second Trianon, Le Trianon de Marbre, on the same site — this time as a home

for his relations with Madame de Maintenon. It was built by Mansart, but Robert de Cotte was responsible for the semicircular peristyle. Tall French windows lead from the rooms into either the gardens or the courtyard. Despite the charm and delicacy of the polychrome marble structure, this château was never very popular with Louis XV or Louis XVI. Napoleon, on the other hand, was very fond of it, while Louis-Philippe housed his daughters there.

Le Petit Trianon is a delightful little square château, decorated with pilasters and columns, designed by the talented Gabriel, which Louis XV built in the park. Marie-Antoinette lived there frequently, with no etiquette. She started by laying out an English park decorated with the Temple of Love built by Mique in the middle of an island. Some distance further on she dug a large lake, on the shores of which a dozen picturesque mud-brick cottages were later built, in keeping with the rustic style in fashion at the moment. This was the Queen's Hamlet, where she played at being a shepherdess. She was there on October 5 1789, when she learnt that the Parisians were marching on Versailles.

Versailles: The "Hamlet" of the Petit Trianon, la Maison de la Reine (the Queen's House), le Moulin (the Mill), close to the gardens. The queen and noble ladies played at being shepherdesses here.

ETIQUETTE

Without Louis XIV's love of pomp and grandeur it would have been impossible to tolerate the austere magnificence of Versailles. His successors arranged more private retreats for themselves, such as the Petits Appartements of Louis XV, those charming rooms on the third and fourth floors, in the attic, with a marvelous view of the lush vegetation of the park. Marie-Antoinette moved into apartments with a southerly exposure which are still known as Les Appartements de la Dauphine.

Louis XIV must have had an extreme sense of rigor in order to devise and institute the countless rules for ceremonial which came to be known as Etiquette, and of which he himself was the first victim. It compelled him to be constantly on parade, or on show, and denied him any solitude whatsoever. The royal Rising and Going to Bed ceremonies were as long as they were tiring. He used to take his meals in front of the assembled court, yet he sat alone at a square table, through

endless meals with what strikes us as mind-boggling menus, including soups (several), *entrées* (several), a number of roasts (for example, two fat capons, nine chickens, nine pigeons, six partridges), tarts (several), two bowls of fruit, two bowls of preserves, two bowls of stewed fruit... And all of that merely for the royal appetite!

On more formal days the sovereign would, as an exception, invite the members of the royal family to join him at his table. On such days he was the host and received his guests bareheaded, whereas his guests had to keep their heads covered.

There were many such caprices of etiquette. "From a reading of the chronicles of the château one fails to understand how everyone, from princes and princesses down to the most anonymous servants managed to cram into their heads and then remember all the minute details of their roles, particularly as those roles changed with the seasons, places and hours." (Le Nôtre) The great ladies were entitled to a stool, a folding chair or a chair with a back, depending on circumstances;

doormen had to stand either inside or outside the doors which it was their duty to open, depending on the circumstances; dukes and peers who were authorized to use a *carreau,* or cushion, in the chapel had to place it slightly sideways, and not straight, like a prince of the blood; the number of steps which one could ascend depended on the rank of the person one was greeting. In other words, etiquette was a constant enslavement.

Under Louis XV it was to become even more severe, as new prohibitions had enriched it over the years. The timid Marie Leczinska and the hot-headed Marie-Antoinette were both to suffer cruelly as a result of it.

Attempts to break out of this intolerable strait-jacket led to the building of the Trianons.

The Versailles ornamental ponds famous for their great fountains. Above right: The most famous of them, by Latone.

FONTAINEBLEAU

Originally Fontainebleau consisted of a hunting lodge built at the edge of a fountain in the Bière Forest —a hunter's paradise— and belonging to the Frankish family known as Blit-Wald. This later evolved to Bliaud or Eblaud.

Several Capetian kings worked on the construction of a fortified manor at this point. Reference is first made to this project in a royal charter from the reign of Louis VII ("the Young"), in 1169. Philippe-Auguste and Saint Louis stayed there many times. Philippe IV ("the Fair") died there from a hunting accident in 1314. Charles V ("the Wise") established a major library there. At the end of the 15th century the castle consisted of a keep and a series of buildings scattered around an oval courtyard. François I was to change all that.

To start with —in keeping with the custom of the period— all these ill-assorted medieval structures were demolished. Then, in 1527, Gilles Le Breton was commissioned to erect a new building. It consisted of two groups of buildings, the one to the east surrounding the Oval Courtyard with its mullioned windows, skylights and huge fireplaces, and the one to the west arranged around the Lower Courtyard which, during the reign of Charles IX, became the Cour du Cheval Blanc ("White Horse Courtyard"), where the monarch erected the plaster statue of a horse cast from that of Marcus-Aurelius at the Capitol. In 1531 these two blocks were linked by a gallery. Work was thereafter directed by the Italian Serlio, who constructed the portico of the Oval Courtyard.

Decoration of the château was entrusted to Rossi and Primaticcio, who had a whole host of artists working under them. Italian influence was predominant at this early stage. These decorators and many of their associates, such as Pellegrini,

Majorici and Nicolo dell'Arbate, were brought back from Italy by François I; Rossi came in 1531 and Primaticcio the following year. During his transalpine campaigns the king was greatly impressed by the charm of the palaces he saw, finding them so different from the grim castles of the French provinces which were often heavily fortified, surrounded by thick walls and deep moats. These artists introduced the French to the techniques of fresco and stucco. We are indebted to Primaticcio for the ceilings and moldings of the François I Gallery, and also for numerous paintings of groups. His paintings for the Ballroom, which later came to be known as Henri II Gallery, have since been restored. The royal apartments which open on to the Oval Courtyard date from this same period.

This first group of artists introduced into France a style influenced by the mannerism of Raphael, Michelangelo, Bronzino and Parmesano. The shapes of the nude figures are more slender, languid and affected. These influences form the first School of Fontainebleau, with Jean Goujon, the two Jean Cousins and Antoine Caron. Allegory was triumphant, with particular emphasis on the image of Diane, so dear to Henri II who, after his father's death, continued the work with Philibert Delorme in charge of operations. The king was particularly fond of Fontainebleau and stayed there often. He commissioned the decor in the Ballroom. In several places a monogram is to be seen: an H, Henri's initial letter, attached to two Cs, C being the initial of Catherine de Médecis, his wife. A closer look, however, reveals a deeper, hidden meaning: the whole combination forms a double D, for Diane de Poitiers, his mistress.

When Henri II was accidentally killed by Montgomery in a tournament, Catherine decided

The château of Fontainebleau is, after Versailles, the most important in the Ile-de-France. Its imposing buildings lie close to the forest. Bottom left: La Cour de la Fontaine (Fountain Courtyard). Right: Two views of the main courtyard with its famous horseshoe-shaped staircase. Following pages: l'Étang des Carpes (the Pool of Carps) and the Louis XV Wing.

that supervision of construction should henceforth be in the hands of her compatriot, Primaticcio and not Philibert Delorme, as before. She and her sons rather neglected Fontainebleau; but under Henri IV, the first Bourbon king, the estate grew considerably. The new prince was to spend more than two million *livres* to embellish it. He was responsible for the new construction around the Cour des Offices ("Pantry Courtyard") —also known as Cour des Cuisines— and the Cour des Princes, as well as the jeu de Paume, the ball court on which he was such an excellent player, and the Baptistry Arch. He completed the execution of plans for the Galerie de Diane. It was during the reign of "good King Henri" that the second Fontainebleau School took form. Triumphant Italianism had now been replaced by the prevalence of Flemish influences: a vigorous yet rather heavy art, occasionally bordering on vulgarity and quite the opposite of the first school.

Louis XIII was born in the salon which bears his same; but Louis XIV was the one who truly appreciated Fontainebleau. It may be because it was where he committed his first act of adultery, in the arms of Louise de La Vallière; twenty years later, the widower of Marie-Thérèse of Austria, he decided, at Fontainebleau, to marry Mme de Maintenon, or Widow Scarron.

The history of the château is well-stocked with events. It was where Christine of Sweden, on November 10 1657, had her Master of the Horse —her lover Monadelschi, apparently— assassinated. Once she had come to her decision, for whatever obscure reasons, she summoned him to

the Galerie des Cerfs to notify him of it, and left him in the company of a priest who heard his confession and of two thugs who slit his throat. In 1685 the Revocation of the Edict of Nantes— a political act with dire consequences— was signed in the apartments of Mme. de Maintenon at the château. Fontainebleau was also the setting, in 1700, for the royal council during which it was decided to accept the will of Charles II of Spain: a Bourbon on the ancient throne of Charles V, and the Pyrenees virtually disappeared!

Under Louis XV the château, and more particularly the royal appartments, was altered. The Royal Staircase was built in what had once been the bedroom of the duchesse d'Etampes, a favorite of François I. Louis XVI doubled the François I Gallery on the north side. With exquisite taste, Marie Antoinette designed a new decor for her apartment. In the old Salon de Jeu ("Gaming Room"), which has remained unchanged, each piece of furniture is an original, only the setting of the room having been restored.

During the Revolution, remarkably enough, the château was not looted, though its furniture was removed. And when the "Corsican with the flat hair" was named first consul he grew fond of the place and therefore had to have it furnished. After

becoming Napoleon he ordered numerous changes in what he called the "house of the centuries". The Galerie de Diane, in particular, needed repair. Later on Napoleon III turned it into a library. Napoleon I turned the bedroom of all the kings of France from Henri IV to Louis XIV into

the Throne Room. He put his own apartments on the first floor —formerly the baths of François I— and the second floor, while Empress Josephine and, later on, Marie-Louise, migrated to rooms around the Salon Jaune on the first floor, with a view of the Jardin de Diane.

The interior of the château of Fontainebleau. Top: Henri II's Ballroom and the King's Room, converted into the Throne Room under Napoleon. Bottom: In the Queen Mother's Apartments, Anne of Austria's room (left) and the salon where the Concordat of 1813 was signed.

Fontainebleau was richly endowed with history during the First Empire. The Treaty on the Partition of Portugal was signed there in 1807. That same year and in 1810 it was there that the emperor signed two decrees to reinforce the Continental Blockade. From 1812 to 1814 The Queen Mothers' Wing was a kind of gilded cage for Pope Pius VII, who was being held in France on the emperor's orders. The pope was no stranger to Fontainebleau, having already been there as visitor in 1804.

It is thought that Napoleon I signed his two abdications, on April 4 and 6 1814 in the Salon Rouge which has since then been known as the Salon de l'Abdication. On the 20th of the same month, in the Cour du Cheval Blanc — which, after the emperor's farewell words, became for many people the Cour des Adieux thereafter— Napoleon, his face flushed and with tears in his eyes, appeared at the top of the Horseshoe Staircase, came down the steps and spoke to his Guard and to the square of officers who surrounded the Eagle: "Continue to serve France, its wellbeing is my only thought... For twenty years... you have always behaved bravely and loyally". He embraced General Petit, kissed the flag and, suddenly turning his back, climbed into the carriage which was to take him to the royal isolation of the island of Elba. Eleven months later, the Eagle flew from one belltower to the next all the way back from there to the towers of Notre-Dame.

Napoleon III was also specially fond of Fontainebleau. He had a small theater built there, from 1854 to 1857, in the Louis XVI style.

In 1949 NATO set up its headquarters at the château, where it stayed until France withdrew from the military command structure of the alliance.

The layout of the gardens has been influenced by a variety of styles. Outside the Cour de la Fontaine, at the entrance to the building, there is a long pond stocked with carp, in the center of which stands a pavilion from the time of Henri IV. An English garden surrounds the fountain, which has given its name to the place. The French-style flowerbeds on the other side of the pond were redesigned by Le Nôtre. Waterfalls, a canal and a huge park bordered on the north by a trellis lie beyond. On the other side of the château, the Jardin de Diane has been altered frequently. The Orangerie which for a while closed its northern end was demolished in the 19th century, to be replaced by specially designed groves. Only the Fontaine de Diane dates from the 17th century.

The domanial forest, which is situated on very uneven terrain, covers a total of 42,500 acres. It includes numerous species of trees; the Scots pine was apparently introduced by the naturalist Lemonnier, the personal physician of Louis XVI.

Fontainebleau. Above: In the forest, the "Table du Roi" (King's Table). Opposite left: An important relic kept in the château, the hat which Napoleon was wearing when he returned from the island of Elba. Right: The ceiling of the Salon des Reines (Queens' Salon).

CHAMPS

Besides being the sinews of war, money is also the driving force of construction. Champs, not very far from Noisy-le-Grand, is a *nouveau riche* residence.

A first rather modest château was built on the site of an old manor house by the treasurer general extraordinary of the wars of Louis XIV, Charles Renouard, who commissioned J.-B. Bullet

The striking thing about this very classical building is that it displays a most unusual sense of the practical comforts of life. The rooms open off a corridor, the bedrooms have a toilet and a wardrobe and some of them have adjacent bathrooms. The kitchens in the basement connect with the pantry near the dining room; and the main drawing room is directly off that room. Such attention to practical matters was doubtless inspired by the new baronness, who keenly remembe-

de Chamblain for the purpose. In 1701, when suddenly plunged into ruinous debt and bankruptcy, Charles Renouard stood on the threshold of his château and saw the bailiffs coming to arrest him. According to the *Mémoires* of Saint-Simon the sight of them made him die of heart failure on the spot.

A second financier bought the estate. Paul Poisson, also known as de Bourvalais, was a self-made man, a former lackey who had made a fortune supplying the armies. In Paris he owned a magnificent private townhouse on the place Vendôme — now the Ministry of Justice. He chose Champs for his country residence because his wife, who had been a servant at the time of their marriage, was a native of the village.

Between 1703 and 1707 he had the same architect who had designed the original pavilion build a three-storey chateau, with fine proportions, around it; it has a centrally located forepart, the entrance to which is in the form of an atrium behind a portico of pilasters and columns.

red her own days as a serving-girl in that same village.

Once he had become a baron, our financier began to give lavish receptions. But not for long. In 1716, during the Regency, he was thrown in jail for embezzlement.

The château, which had been confiscated by the Crown, was bought by the princesse de Conti, the natural daughter of Louis XIV and Mlle de La Vallière, who ceded it to her nephew, the duc de La Vallière. The duke had a young relative of Le Nôtre, Claude Desgots, design a magnificient park in the French style, descending through a succession of levels, with flower beds and copses, towards the left bank of the Marne. He also decorated the salon and a boudoir, around 1740, with *chinoiseries* and *singeries,* in polychrome and blue monochrome, respectively.

Rising expenses, however, forced the duke to rent his property to Madame de Pompadour, whose maiden name was also, curiously enough, Poisson. She paneled her room with wood carvings of the loves of two doves, and decorated a bathroom with stucco in the antique style.

The château passed through a succession of owners —including the marquise de Marbeuf, who was beheaded in 1794 — before being acquired in 1895 by comte Cahen d'Anvers, whose son gave the property to the State in 1935. It is now used as the summer residence of the president ot the Council of Ministers.

The château de Champs and its French gardens, at a succession of different levels. Opposite right: Le Jardin de Madame (Madame's Garden) and one of the salons.

Between 1656 and 1659 Superintendent Nicolas Fouquet built on his estate at Vaux a château worthy of his fortune and his ambition. Starting out at the age of twenty as a member of the Parliament of Paris, by 1650 he had become the city's prosecutor general and a friend of Mazarin. Originally associated with Servien as superintendent of finance, he held the post alone by 1659 and acquired a huge fortune, often confusing his own accounts with those of the kingdom, rather like his friend the cardinal. This madly ambitious man adopted the motto *Quo non ascendam?* ("How far shall I not rise?") and acquired the viscountship of Melun. Then he brought in the greatest artists of his day —the architect Le Vau, the decorator Le Brun, the architect and landscape artist Le Nôtre— and in five years, with eighteen thousand men on the job, he built one of the purest gems of 17th-century architecture.

The château, which is situated at the top of a small number of steps and surrounded by moats, has three levels of differing heights, the reception floor having very high ceilings; the central residential section is crowned by a dome, with two offset lateral pavilions. On the inside, an oval drawing room decorated with twelve cariatids directly below the dome was never completed; it leads to two rows of apartments, including four formal reception rooms. Fouquet, who was an enlightened collector and a fabulous patron of the arts, set up a library of thirteen thousand volumes and a number of sumptuous collections. Le Brun painted portraits and produced remarkable decors for him; he also built a tapestry studio at Maincy which, when later moved to Paris, combined with the Gobelins to become the Royal Factory. Fouquet protected Poussin, Puget, Girardon, Legendre and, in another sphere, Molière and La Fontaine. The loyal fable-writer returned this friendship in due course by protecting his protector in his *Elegy to the Nymphs of Vaux.*

Le Nôtre's quite exceptional gardens make use

of the natural slope of the land to create some surprise effects. The eye is treated to a succession of long ponds, a grand canal and French-style flower beds reaching as far as the niches decorated with rock-work which are known as Les Grottes. Both the residence and the park are straight out of a dream. In the words of the historian Georges Lenôtre: "Where there had

once been only rabbit warrens, fields, marshes and moors, we now see disciplined woods, limpid waters falling in cascades or rising in sheaves, carpets of smooth grass, statues aligned in the

Vaux-le-Vicomte. Its impressive park and the three-level constructions. Right: The Large Salon.

shade of the arbors, and, overlooking this lush Garden of Eden, a palace whose grand yet appealing façades stand on a pedestal of terraces in the midst of marble and flowers".

Of course the entire court was eager to see this marvel for itself — particularly Louis XIV. So he virtually demanded an invitation from his superintendent, while he was staying at Fontainebleau. Fouquet, overwhelmed with pride, organized a lavish celebration in the king's honor on August 17 1661. Construction, however, was not yet finished and the residence contained little furniture. Yet the need to satisfy the monarch prevailed over all else. Fouquet went to immense trouble to organize the meals, the bedrooms and the entertainment. He stripped his houses in Paris and Saint-Mandé of their furniture, tableware, carpets and tapestries. He unceasingly urged the workers, gardeners and painters to greater efforts. He commissioned a play, *Les Fâcheux*, from Molière. He arranged for rustic dances, and hired the famous pyrotechnic experts Giacomo Torelli to devise a firework display, the likes of which had never been seen before. An army of cooks, kitchen boys and pastry cooks toiled away under the orders of his famous *maître d'hôtel*, Vatel. The king's meal was to be served on gold tableware.

At last the great day arrived. "Overcome with fatigue and burning with fever, a smiling Fouquet was in ecstasy as he received his guests. The embarrassment began, however, as soon as he greeted the king. At a glance the young monarch had sized up the wonders which awaited him; he had never seen anything so beautiful, and he did not like what he saw at all" (Le Nôtre). He compared the fortune of his superintendent of finance to his own dire straits. Had he not just been forced to melt down his tableware to meet the costs arising out of the Thirty Years' War? He was all the more furious in that Colbert had, for some months past, been denouncing the embezzlement committed so often by Fouquet.

The very day of the reception, Louis decided to have his superintendent arrested. The queen mother, Anne of Austria, talked him out of it. Even so, he was exceedingly frigid and aloof as he sat through the entertainment and tasted the most sophisticated of dishes, the freshest of fish; when evening came he refused to spend the night in the apartment which had been set aside for him and went back to Fontainebleau. Fouquet sensed the chill wind which was blowing his way and decided to give to the Crown the fortress of Belle-Isle-en-Mer, which was his property.

To no avail: nineteen days later he was arrested at Nantes (by d'Artagnan, a future field marshal, but then an officer in the Corps of Grey Musketeers). He was put on trial for embezzlement and conspiracy (his archives were found to contain plans, dated 1657, for resistance at his Belle-Isle fortress, in case of trouble), and sentenced to perpetual banishment and the confiscation of his property. Louis XIV aggravated the penalty by converting it into detention for life in the fortress of Pignerol, where Fouquet died in 1680.

Vaux is a sort of small younger brother of the château of Versailles, for two reasons: Louis XIV was determined to make his residence even more sumptuous, and he happened to hire all the artists who had been discovered by Fouquet.

Vaux-le-Vicomte. Left: The King's apartement and the Hercules Salon. On this page: The library and the sideboard of the former dining-room of the intendant Fouquet, for whom this noble dwelling was erected, the inspiration for Versailles.

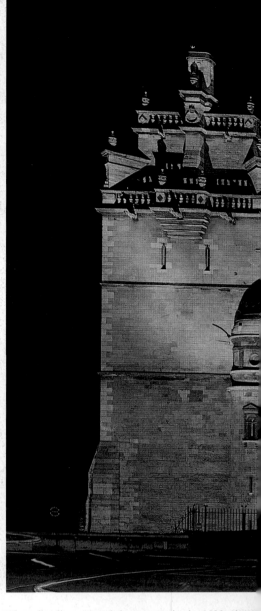

SAINT-GERMAIN-EN-LAYE

The château of Saint-Germain, situated in the ancient forest of Laye, can be traced back to a fortress built by Louis VI ("the Fat"), between 1122 and 1124, on the strategic site of Saint-Germain Hill. In 1230 Louis IX — in keeping perhaps with his saintly attributes — added the chapel which still exists today; its elegant nave with pointed arches was probably the work of Pierre de Montreuil. During the Hundred Years' War the château was partially destroyed, after the fire started by the Anglo-Burgundian forces, yet the Sainte Chapelle miraculously escaped the flames. In 1367 Charles V ("the Wise") rebuilt the castle, with a square keep, which the English were to recapture in 1419. They were driven out in 1440 by Constable de Richemont.

In 1514 Claude de France, the daughter of Henri II — who has given her name to a species of plum — married, in the Sainte Chapelle, her cousin François d'Angoulême who, one year later, was to ascend the throne of France as François I. At first François I neglected Saint-Germain, preferring the milder banks of the Loire. It was only after his return from captivity in Madrid, after the disastrous defeat at Pavia, in 1528, that he decided to settle in and around Paris, as a way of thanking the people of Paris for their part in raising his ransom. In 1539 he commissioned Pierre de Chambiges, who had already been involved in work at Chantilly, to build a new château. He was followed by his son-in-law Guillaume Guillain. With the exception of the keep and the chapel, the old castle was demolished, and a new fortress rose in its place. It was decided to preserve, as had been the case at Chantilly, the irregular pentagonal plan and the foundations of two stone stories overlooking the ditches, forming the old machicolated walkway. Chambiges contructed two more floors using a mixture of stone and brick, with pilasters, semi-circular arch windows, and triangular pediments very much in the sober manner of the second half of François I's reign. The keep was rejuvenated by the same balustrades that ran along the roof of the château. It was possible to walk around on these terraces; but, despite this Italian innovation, there are round turrets at the corners of the outer perimeter. The rooms have Gothic arches because of the weight of the terraces; for that reason the salient buttresses had to be built on the courtyard façades in order to support the arches.

This new building was where François spent his last year. A famous duel took place that same year on the esplanade, between François de Vivonne,

Saint-Germain-en-Laye. Its arched windows are in exactly the style of the second half of the reign of François I.

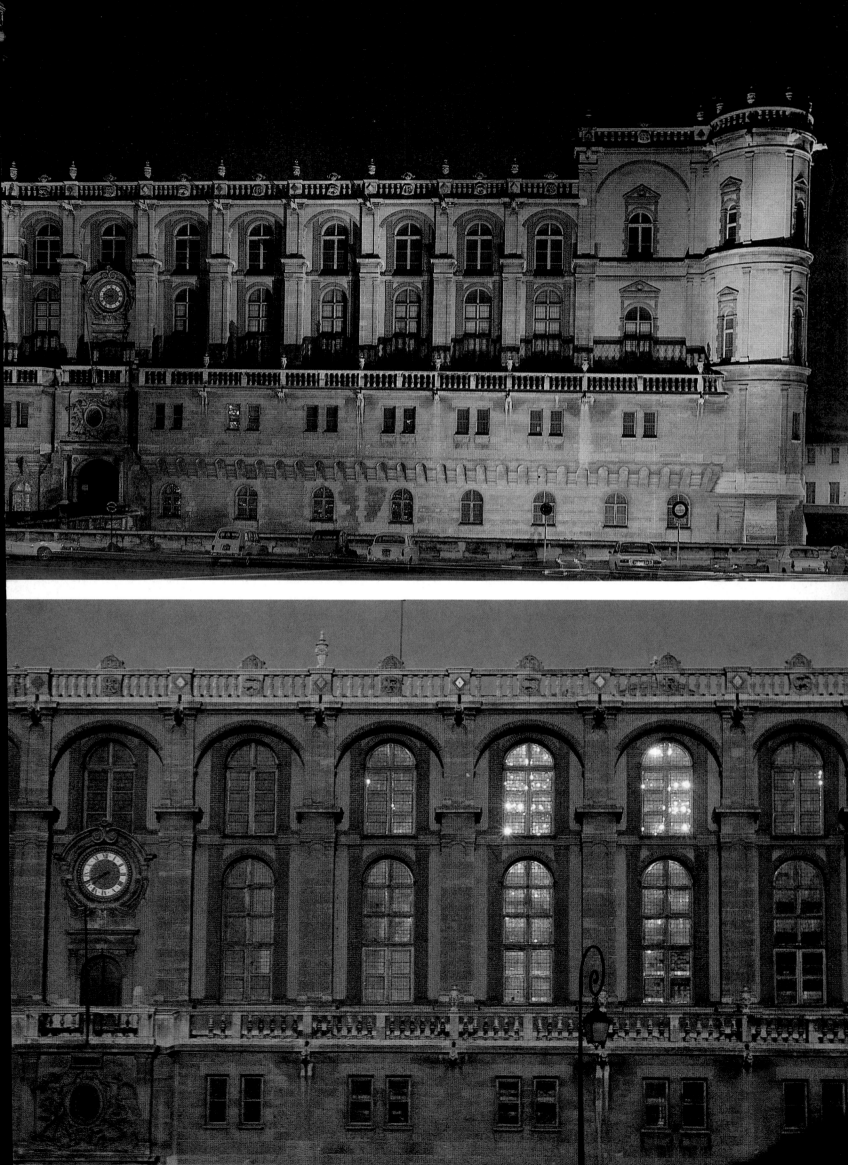

lord of La Châtaigneraie and a dreaded swash-buckler, and Guy Chabot, baron de Jarnac. By means of a perfectly fair but unexpect blow on the ham the baron overcame his dangerous adversary: his technique was later immortalized in the expression *coup de Jarnac*.

Henri II, who was born at Saint-Germain, found the place too heavily fortified and commissioned Philibert Delorme to erect a pleasure building which would be both "theater and baths". This Château Neuf rose on the edge of the plateau, formed of two buildings in the shape of a cross, with pavilions and galleries. Work continued under the guidance of Primaticcio but was not completed until the time of Henri IV. Catherine de Médicis, who had become so influential in her roles as regent and queen mother, refused to live there after someone had predicted that she would die near Saint Germain. The prediction actually came true, but the Saint Germain in question was a man, the priest who attended her on her deathbed! And then the wars of religion which were in full swing were not conducive to new building projects. However, Mary Stuart was raised there, from the age of six to sixteen, awaiting her glorious and tragic destiny.

It was therefore Henri IV who commissioned the architect Louis Métézeau and the master mason Guillaume Marchant to complete the construction. The most striking feature of Saint-Germain is the succession of terraces, of arcaded walls, of courtyards and double staircases which descend towards the Seine, very much in the Italian style. Grottoes clad in rocks and inhabited by automatic devices were built next to the foundations. In them Orpheus played music, the animals came close to listen and Neptune's chariot advanced majestically. These devices were powered by a hydraulic mechanism built by the Francines, the Italian engineers, father and son, who also produced the fountains at Versailles. Henri IV occasionally enjoyed sprinkling his guests from hidden nozzles. The mural decor of one of these grottoes still exists in the lower part of the Henri IV Pavilion. In the room above, which was then the Oratory, the future Louis XIV, who was born at the château, was baptized privately before his ceremonial baptism in 1643 in the Sainte Chapelle. During the Fronde, Anne of Austria took refuge there with the adolescent king and Mazarin, in great discomfort. Then the court came frequently to Saint-Germain, either to the Château Neuf or the Château Vieux.

The number of diplomatic instruments which were signed at Saint-Germain makes it clear that the king and his ministers must have stayed there for quite a long time on each visit. They include: the edict of 1570 authorizing the Huguenots to practise their form of worship; the 1639 declaration in which Louis XIII reminded the French clergy of the precarious nature of property held in mortmain; the 1641 edict which enabled Richelieu to foil the Parliament; and several treaties with foreign powers. Louis XIII died at Saint-Germain. Henriette de France, wife of Charles I of England, stayed there with her two sons while her husband was making one last, vain attempt to save his throne and his head. The English monarchy was restored, and the two princes were to reign successively, but the younger one, James II, was forced to abdicate. When sent into exile he went to Saint-Germain, where he was received with the greatest deference by Louis XIV and where he

lived out the rest of his life.

In the meantime Saint-Germain had a period of great merrymaking, as the Sun-King gave some brilliant receptions there. Molière came with his troupe of actors, Le Vau produced a new decor, Le Nôtre developed the terrace along the edge of the forest and improved the landscape at this point by planting five and a half million young trees. Mansart, in 1676, enlarged the Château Vieux by adding five pavilions replacing the corner turrets.

Saint-Germain's heyday came to an end with the construction of the new palace at Versailles. Louis XIV lost interest in it. As we have seen, the Château Vieux served as accommodation for his cousin James II of England, who lived an extremely modest and retiring life while he was there. The Château Neuf, which was uninhabited, gradually deteriorated until it was only a ruin.

Louis XVI sold it to his brother the comte d'Artois, the future Charles X, who demolished all

the buildings except the two pavilions of Sully and Henri IV. But he soon shelved his plans for further construction and turned instead to work on the enlargement of Maisons, the future Maisons-Laffitte.

The Revolution aggravated the disaster. Napoleon established a school of cavalry in the Château Vieux, while Louis-Philippe used it as a military penitentiary. Napoleon commissioned the architect Millet to carry out restoration work on the Château Vieux. He razed Mansart's five pavilions, and reconstructed the building according to the plans of François I, in the Renaissance style. But Saint-Germain's best days were over. In 1867 the emperor converted it into the Musée des Antiquités Nationales.

One last treaty was signed in 1919 at Saint-Germain by the Allied Powers and the new Republic of Austria — a treaty which confirmed the collapse of the Austro-Hungarian monarchy of the Habsburgs.

MAISONS-LAFFITTE

Maisons provides a magnificent illustration of the new fortunes acquired by the legal profession in the 17th century: the Longueil family had owned for two centuries a huge estate between the forest of Saint-Germain and the left bank of the Seine, where a rather modest manor house stood. Under Louis XIII, René de Longueil was president of the Paris Parliament, governor of the châteaux of Versailles and Saint-Germain, captain of the Royal Hunt and even superintendent of finance. It was not surprising that he should have accumulated great wealth. He was so busy that he kept this last post for only one year, saying plaintively at the end: "They were wrong to dismiss me; I had done my own business — did they expect me to do theirs?".

His business thus completed he commissioned François Mansart in 1642 to replace the family manor with an impressive residence — particularly bearing in mind that the sovereign had the right to stay at Maisons when he chose. Construction lasted nine years. The very classical building thus

produced consists of a long central section flanked by two pavilions, with a prominently protruding fore-part in the center. The steeply sloping roofs bristle with tall chimneys. Mansart decided to avoid using brick and relied solely on cut stone. He organized the three levels of the building according to the Doric order which was used on the first floor, the Ionic on the second and the Corinthian on the third.

The external splendor of the place was certainly matched on the inside, which included a ceremonial stone and stucco staircase with an indented banister, a vestibule adorned with sculptures in the round, pilasters and Doric columns. The second floor contained the royal apartments which Louis XIV was to inaugurate. At the time he was aged thirteen, but he returned to Maisons several times, and after him came Louis XV and Louis XVI. The interior of the château was renovated several times, particularly the principal apartments of the owners. The great-grandson of René de Longueil, a keen scientist, built a laboratory there.

Views of the château of Maisons-Laffitte; an architectural detail. Right: The small salon and the bedroom which Louis XIV used for the first time.

On the whole the château was suffering from neglect when it was sold in 1777 to the comte d'Artois, the future Charles X, who, being greatly influenced by things English, established a kitchen garden and built two dining rooms — a typical innovation. Being a devoted horse-racer, he restored the stables.

Unfortunately the château, which was confiscated under the property laws of the Revolution and acquired in 1804 by Marshal Lannes, was eventually sold by the widow of the hero of Essling to the banker Laffitte, in 1818. Business being business, the banker had the park subdivided and demolished the superb stables built by Mansart—and then sold off the building materials at rock-bottom prices! The new estate took the name of its "promoter": Maisons-Laffitte.

The château suffered cruelly as a result of this amputation of its magnificent environment. When threatened with demolition it was bought in 1905 by the State. For many years it was an annex to the French National Museums, and is now attached to the Administration of Historic Monuments.

MARLY-LE-ROI

There is nothing left of the château of Marly. A visitor walking through the restored gardens today would simply have to visualize for himself the kind of residence that the Sun-King called his "hermitage".

Abreuvoir (literally, "drinking-trough"), an immense trapezoidal pond which acts as a weir and on the banks of which, in 1702, two groups of equestrian statues by Coysevox were placed.

Louis XIV was personally the *deus ex machina* of Marly. He made it his haven of peace—relatively speaking, of course. He loved to stay

gardens and replaced by the famous groups by Guillaume Coustou now known as the *Horses of Marly*. At present they form a frame for the view along the Champs-Elysees.

In 1728 the Great Waterfall, which Cardinal Fleury found too expensive to maintain, was replaced by the lawn which covers the site today.

Shortly after the Treaty of Nimègue, which left Louis XIV the arbiter of all Europe, the king decided to commission Mansart to build for him at Marly a small château specially designed for relaxation, far from the etiquette which he himself had imposed at Versailles. Actually, it was to be not so much a château as a cluster of pavilions in a highly original style devised to illustrate the theme of the Sun-King. The central building—obviously that of the king— towers over two parallel rows of six pavilions each (symbolizing the solar system) which were reserved for guests. The royal quarters, flanked by the pavilion of the guards and the chapel, is cubic, in the style of the Italian Palladio; four vestibules in the shape of a Greek cross lead to four apartments from a central polygonal drawing room. The roofs are hidden behind a balustrade; pilasters mingle with Baroque themes, painted, for reasons of economy, in *trompe-l'œil*.

The park, designed by Le Nôtre, opens with a truly regal view of the nearby forest. To the south, between masses of moss and greenery, a long waterfall flows from the top of the hill down fifty-two pink marble steps, past statues on mythological themes, rock gardens and porticoes. Northwards, beyond a long expanse of water, is the

there often, with his family and a few friends. Over a period of thirty years, he did not invite more than about eight hundred noblemen and three hundred ladies. Accomodation was limited, with only two apartments per pavilion, for a total of twenty-four. Those privileged enough to be invited obviously vied with one another for the honor of having a bedroom as close as possible to the king. Etiquette was greatly relaxed at Marly. The king dined with his guests; the assembled company played cards, danced, listened to concerts, went hunting and took walks. It was not, however, a very comfortable place, especially from the point of view of heating. Despite the improvements devised each year by Louis XIV, everyone shivered in winter, and the smoke was appaling as the humidity prevented the fireplaces from drawing properly. In summer malaria was a real danger. But who cared? The entire court dreamed of securing an invitation to Marly.

On August 9 1715 the king, at the age of seventy-seven, had been out following the hunt in a carriage. Suddenly he felt so tired that he was taken back to Versailles, where he died shortly afterwards.

Under the Regency, in 1719, Coysevox's statues were transported to the entrance to the Tuileries

Louis occasionally went to Marly when in a dejected mood. As Louis XVI neglected the place altogether it was gradually looted. The furniture was sold off cheaply during the Revolution.

In 1800 the château was bought by a M. Sagniel who established a textile factory in the royal pavilion and a spinning mill in the outbuildings. The courtiers of the Sun-King were now replaced by some three hundred and fifty workers. But business went downhill. When bankruptcy threatened our financier offered the estate to Napoleon in 1806. The emperor declined. Then Sagniel demolished all the buildings except for the kennels and sold off the materials and then the land for whatever he could get. A year later, the new owner ceded the property to the emperor. Marly became State property and remained abandoned for decades. Nowadays the gardens have been partly restored, much to the satisfaction of the general public.

Different views of the beautiful park, rich in history, of Marly-le-Roi and the remains of the château.

RAMBOUILLET

As early as the Carolingian period there was a manor/hunting lodge in the Yvelines Forest. In 1374 Jehan Bernier, provost of the merchants of Paris, and later a member of the Regency Council of Charles VI after the monarch's insanity, bought the property. The new owner built a triangular castle surrounded by moats and flanked at its three corners by slender round towers. Ten years later, after his father's death, Guillaume Bernier sold the fortress to Regnault d'Angennes, a member of a family from the Perche. The estate remained the property of the family until the reign of Louis XIV.

The construction of a large round tower and of two smaller towers in front of it, between 1406 and 1413, gave the building the pentagonal

appearance which it was to retain for many years, despite numerous alterations over the centuries. The large tower is now the only part of the castle which is still more or less in its original condition; the others have been much renovated. The outer walls were demolished and rebuilt a number of times, starting in the first half of the 15th century. During the Hundred Years' War the castle suffered a great deal of damage. Napoleon destroyed the left wing and replaced the original pentagon with an L-shape.

Rambouillet has always been prime hunting territory, and accordingly it was a favorite with the kings of France, all of them to varying degrees dedicated to the hunt, who stayed there frequently, François I went there in 1547. At the time the owner was Jacques d'Angennes, captain of the Gardes du Corps. On returning from a hunting

sortie, the king was taken ill, went to bed and died shortly afterwards. His son and successor, Henri II was also a frequent visitor, and Jacques d'Angennes had the château duly embellished for these royal visits.

In 1600 Charles d'Angennes, Jacques' Grandson, married Catherine de Vivonne, a descendant, through her mother, of an illustrious Roman family.

She was only twelve years old, but was already graceful, cultivated and witty. At quite an early age she began to entertain - and entertain well - even more at her Paris townhouse than in the château, the estate of which was elevated to the rank of marquisate in 1612. Catherine became the very famous marquise de Rambouillet, the best known of the précieuses—the one whom Malherbe chose to name *Arthénice* (anagram of Catherine), and, whom Fléchigr called 'the incomparable Arthénice'. It was she who devised the notion of forming a union of ladies and gentlemen of high birth, churchmen and men of letters in order to fight the coarseness of manners and language which had prevailed at the court since Henri IV. Her guests included the duchesse de La Trémoille, the duchesse de Longueville, Mademoiselle de Scudéry, the prince de Condé, the duc d'Enghien his son, Richelieu, Bossuet, Racan, Vaugelas, Chape-

The château of Rambouillet and its majestic setting. Opposite left: The English garden.

lain, Voiture, Scarron and Corneille. One can truly say that, thanks to her efforts, the French literary scene was to take a new turn and that *l'honnête parler,* a style of writing on which the 17th century prided itself, was to some extent her handiwork. In *Le Grand Cyrus,* Georges and Madeleine de Scudéry, in the person of Cleomire, drew the following portrait of the marquise de Rambouillet: "Imagine Beauty itself, if you would conceive that of this admirable woman; moreover, she is such a marvel that her wit and her soul both clearly surpass even her beauty".

La Guirlande de Julie (Julie's Garland), one of the masterpieces of *précieuse* literature, consists of sixty-one poems written in honor of her daughter, Julie d'Angennes, by relatives of the marquise. Julie kept the marquis de Montausier—whom Molière is said to have portrayed as Alceste in *Le Misanthrope*—waiting thirteen years before agreeing to marry him.

The marquis de Montausier was the first to have canals dug in the grounds of the château, thus greatly enhancing its charm. In 1799 the estate was sold to the financier Fleuriau d'Ermenonville, who rebuilt the outbuildings, dug the Grand Canal in the shape of a T and greatly

altered the park by placing numerous statues in it. He was just about to demolish the old château, to replace it with something more modern, when Louis XIV, in 1706, obliged him to sell it to him, in return for a handsome compensation, as a residence for the comte de Toulouse, one of the illegitimate—but legitimized—sons he had by Madame de Montespan.

The new owner drastically altered the park by adding a series of canals forming a crow's foot with that built by Fleuriau d'Ermenonville, and added two wings closing off the sides of the main courtyard. Then, during the reign of Louis XV, the comte de Toulouse, the better to receive those invited to the royal hunt, attached to the west wing, on the park side, a building consisting of superb drawing rooms with splendid carved oak wood paneling—which is now unfortunately in a sorry state. His son, the duc de Penthièvre, built a delightful bathroom lined with Delft tiles on the ground floor, had an English garden laid out in 1779, and built, for his daughter-in-law, the princesse de Lamballe, the Pavillon des Coquillages, the exterior of which looks like a cottage, while the interior is curiously clad in colored stones and seashells (coquillages). One can only feel sorry for the

princesse de Lamballe! As a friend of Marie-Antoinette, and detested quite as universally, her head impaled on the end of a pike was brought before the queen outside the windows of the Temple, in September 1792.

Nine years later Louis XVI had bought Rambouillet with the intention of having it rebuilt for his wife. However, on account of the endemically poor state of his finances, he abandoned this project, and was content to build one small building, La Laiterie (dairy) in the park. This very sophisticated dairy, which was designed by Tévenin, is in the neo-classical style; a fine interior rotonda is entirely clad in marble and crowned by a cupola of caissons forming a glass roof; the entrance pavilion is decorated with grisailles producing optical illusions; a very beautiful statue by Julien, *The Nymph with the Goat,* stands in a grotto.

Then came 1793, and the château was turned into a prison—very much a sign of the times. The furniture was sold off cheaply. During the Empire, Napoleon restored the estate, but demolished the east wing. A bathroom in the Pompeian style was built for him in the west wing. In 1814 Marie-Louise was host to her father, Emperor Francis II of Austria, at Rambouillet. In 1815 the victorious troops of the Allies occupied the château, much to its disadvantage. Later on Charles X made some not very successful alterations to the façades. In 1830 Rambouillet was where the last Bourbon king signed his act of abdication. His successor, Louis-Philippe, left the château in an abandoned state, but the Third Republic, during the seven-year term of Felix Faure, restored it for use as the head of State's summer residence.

The experimental farm, which later became the Bergerie Nationale, was founded by Louis XVI, who imported the first merino sheep from Spain. It is part of the Rambouillet Center for Zootechnical Studies.

The interior of the château of Rambouillet: A decorative motif, the room called the "Chaumière des Coquillages" (The Shell Cottage) and, right, a detail of its decoration. Opposite left: La Salle des Marbres (The Marble Room).

DAMPIERRE

On his return from captivity in Spain, François I fell in love with a maid of honor in the service of his mother, Louise de Savoie. Her name was Anne de Pisseleu. In 1533 he married her to Jean des Brosses, whom he made, for the occasion, duc d'Etampes and governor of Brittany. The new duke owned a lordship *(seigneurie)* in the valley of Chevreuse which was to be elevated to the rank of marquisate in 1545 and later to that of duchy. The château de la Madeleine, the feudal castle built by Robert the Pious in the 10th century on this estate is still partly standing

Around 1675 he built yet another château, designed by Jules Hardouin Mansart, and which was one of the largest privates residences of the period. Curiously, the site chosen for this huge structure is situated against the background of a hillside, along which Le Nôtre laid out splendid gardens in the French style. Another unusual

today.

In 1552 this land was acquired by Cardinal Charles de Lorraine, who, feeling little inclination for embarking on the restoration of this forbidding fortress, bought a nearby manor belonging to Treasurer Jean Duvalèt and built in its place a sumptuous château in the Renaissance style. The cardinal died in 1574 at Avignon, leaving his property to his nephew, Henri I de Lorraine, duc de Guise, popularly known as 'Scarface', on account of a facial wound. After the duke's assassination at Blois, his widow retired to Dampierre.

In 1557 the estate was inherited by the widow of his son Claude, who had died childless. She was known more particularly in history as the duchesse de Chevreuse. Her life was a tangled web of amorous and political adventures, as she took part in countless conspiracies and had an equally countless number of lovers. To begin with she was exiled do Dampierre by Richelieu (who demolished the château de la Madeleine), took part in the Fronde and found herself exiled yet again—this time by Mazarin—to Dampierre. In 1663 she gave the estate to her son Charles Albert, duc de Luynes, who had been born of her first marriage. Her grandson Charles Honore, Colbert's son-in-law, decided to order the demolition of the château of the Cardinal de Lorraine, except for certain parts of the outbuildings which still remain standing.

feature: the brick which outlines the roughcast masonry sections is the principal material used. The overall effect is rather like that of Versailles. Two stories are situated over a service basement, the windows of which look out over the moats of the rear façade, which are crossed by a monumental staircase chapel like a bridge. Light enters the attic through skylights and Mansard-style bull's-eyes.

Charles Honore's grandson, Charles Philippe, had the ground floor of the house decorated with magnificent white paneling which is still in excellent condition. During the 19th century Durban had the building restored, choosing to decorate the upper floor in the neo-antique style.

The château which is still in the possession of the de Luyens family houses a considerable number of sumptuous collections, including a fine silver statue of Louis XIII by Rude, and even a model of the well-known *Athena* of Phidias, by Simart.

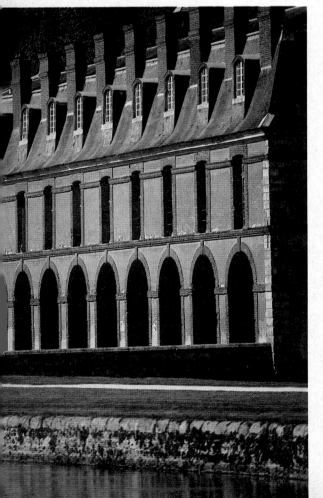

Various views of the château of Dampierre, scene of the amorous and political adventures of the Duchess of Chevreuse.

MALMAISON

In 1622 a councillor in the Parliament, Christophe Perrot, built a rather modest château, consisting of a main dwelling flanked by two pavilions with pointed roofs, on a piece of land which had once belonged to the Abbey of Saint-Denis. Its name, Malmaison, (literally "bad house") was doubtless a reminder of a lepers' hospital which must have stood on the site in medieval times.

In 1771 the financier Lecoulteux du Moley added some sparkle to the place by setting up a literary and artistic salon whose regular guests included Madame Vigée-Lebrun — the favorite painter of Marie-Antoinette — and Abbé Dellile, who showed remarkable courage by daring to translate Virgil into French verse. Josephine de Beauharnais also visited Malmaison: she took a liking to it and, three years after her marriage to Bonaparte, while the general was away campaigning in Egypt, she bought the property... without being completely sure how she was to pay for it.

Percier and Fontaine were brought in to restore the building, which was in very poor condition. In order to strengthen it structurally they built buttresses in the form of Doric pilasters bearing vases and statues, in the neo-antique style of the day. They added to the main entrance a veranda shaped like an army tent, and flanked the building with two small wings. The Jacob brothers

La Malmaison (The Bad House), so called probably after a medieval leper hospital. It was bought by Joséphine de Beauharnais three years after her marriage to Bonaparte and later restored by her.

made a set of superb furniture for Josephine; indeed it is still possible to see their library, with its mahogany columns and domed ceiling decorated with paintings in the Pompeian style.

Josephine moved into Malmaison from her small Paris townhouse on rue Chantereine. On her return from Italy she brought with her a charming captain named Charles who, in the words of Georges Lenôtre, was "short, but well-built, handsome, lively and witty, with a ready stock of puns and an entertaining presence". While Bonaparte was away in the army Charles was Josephine's preferred guest. She continued to invite him to her house when Bonaparte was in Egypt; and remained on intimate terms with him, thus scandalizing her peasants, when she bought the château of Malmaison.

When Bonaparte returned from Egypt, where he had been informed of his wife's infidelity, the townhouse on the rue Chantereine came close to being the scene of the death of the love-story of Josephine and her "puss in boots". However, after she had spent an entire night sobbing outside a door which remained solidly closed, he at last opened it and she threw herself into his arms. According to Lenôtre, her love for Bonaparte truly began on that day.

He paid his wife's debts and soon came to fall in love with Malmaison himself. During the Consulat he lived and worked there quite often. The renovation of the Salle du Conseil in the form of a tent was done for his benefit. Once he had become emperor, Napoleon spent more time in residence at Saint-Claude than at Malmaison, which he found rather too small; but it continued,

nonetheless, to be Josephine's favorite residence.

When they divorced, she chose it as her home. On December 15 1809, Josephine went through a most traumatic experience: she had to read out her renunciation of the crown, before the assembled court. "With the permission of our august and cherished spouse, I must declare that, having no further hope of having children who might satisfy his political needs and the interests of France..." Emotion overcame her and she could not go on; Regnault took the text from her hands and finished reading it. The paper from which she read is now in the National Archives of France. Some parts of it seem to have been stained, perhaps by tears.

The very next day, in her fine carriage, all gilded and draped with heavy fringes, which was known as the Opal (now in the Musée de Trianon), she set off for Malmaison. It was a gloomy, rainy day, almost as if nature itself was weeping with the banished empress.

In purely material terms, however, the emperor treated his first wife sumptuously. She retained the title of empress with her own house and court. Not only did she keep Malmaison as her summer residence, but the emperor also offered her the Palais de l'Elysée in Paris and paid all her debts, which ran into millions of francs. Shortly afterwards, he gave her the château of Navarre, near Evreux, together with its estate. But Josephine grew bored, and the retinue of the deposed former First Lady grew bored with her. The jealousy of Marie-Louise, from 1810 onwards, was such that she was advised to stay away from the Paris which so enchanted her. The Elysée was taken away

from her, and the château de Laeken, near Brussels, was offered in compensation. Even Malmaison was too close. She wandered from one fashionable spa to the next.

Meanwhile, the wheel of fortune was turning. The emperor abdicated. Foreign soldiers camped in Paris. The Bourbons made their return. What was to happen to the ex-wife of the 'Ogre of Corsica'? Was she to be reduced to the life of a beggar, her dowry and endowment stripped from her? Curiously enough, she was not. The new masters of Paris showed sympathy to the woman who had been spurned by the 'Usurper'. Moreover, their curiosity aroused, they were anxious to make the acquaintance of a central figure in one of the greatest adventures of history. The tsar visited her at Malmaison.

She was left Navarre and her beloved Malmaison. Her salon was extremely well attended, being frequented by the tsar twice a week. King Louis XVIII invited her to the Tuileries for the celebrations of May 28 1814. But she was fated never to return to the palace which she had left in tears, four and a half years earlier. On May 25 she developed a sore throat, by the 26th she was shivering from fever, on the 28th her situation became critical, and on the 29th she breathed her last.

Napoleon was on the island of Elba. He learnt of the death of the woman he had loved so much by reading the newspaper. Malmaison then entered a period of mourning. Hortense de Beauharnais, Josephine's daughter, ex-queen of Holland lived there in the midst of the family's shadows. Napoleon returned one last time to Malmaison

just after Waterloo, and shortly before his departure for the island of Aix, from June 25 to 29 1815. While he was there he recovered the memory of the woman to whom he had so often said, holding her in his arms: "My poor Josephine, I shall never be able to manage without you!" After that he went to Saint Helena.

Hortense left the house, with all its phantoms, and her brother Eugene, inherited it. He kept the property until his death, but his widow sold it with all its furniture, which was thereafter scattered far and wide. From 1829 onwards the property passed to a succession of owners: an assortment of bankers, one of them Swedish, the queen of Spain, Napoleon III and several others acquired Malmaison and gradually let it slide into ruin. Lastly, a philanthropic financier by the name of Osiris bought the property and made a gift of it to the State. Some years later Malmaison was turned into a national museum devoted to the memory of Napoleon. Since then it has been an international place of pilgrimage. More than any other place in which the emperor's memory lingers on, this house is haunted by the shadows of the love between a frail Creole girl and a slender thirty-year-old general.

La Malmaison. Top right: Joséphine's apartments. (bottom): Napoleon's salon. Following pages: The château and its buttresses, consisting of Doric pilasters surmounted by vases and statues.

SAINT-CLOUD

Clodoald, son of Clodomir, the second son of Clovis and Clotilde, and Frankish king of Orléans from 511 to 524, gave his name to Saint-Cloud.

During the 15th century a large number of fine residences were built in this area, particularly the mansion of a Parisian notable, Jehan Rouille — the Hotel d'Aulnay. Catherine de Medicis bought it in 1577 as a gift for one of her councillors, her Florentine compatriot Gondi. Henri III was there on August 1, 1589, just about to lay siege to Paris, when he was assassinated by the 'made monk', Jacques Clément.

The property remained in the Gondi family. In 1625 its owner, Jean-François de Gondi — the first archbishop of Paris, which had hitherto been a mere bishopric — commissioned Lepautre to beautify the place. He laid out Italian-style gardens between the house and the Seine, with a grotto as was customary during that period.

In 1655 Philippe d'Orleans, the king's brother, bought the estate and brought in Le Nôtre to work on the gardens. His first wife, Henrietta of England, died there suddenly in 1670. He later replaced the Gondi's house by a large three-floor chateau built by Jules Hardouin-Mansart and Jean Girard and decorated by Mignard and Nocret. Saint-Cloud continued to be the residence of the Orleans family for more than a century. The regent lived and entertained there. His guests included none other than Peter the Great, tsar of all Russia.

In 1785 Louis XVI bought the château as a gift for his wife Marie-Antoinette, who had it restored by Richard and superbly furnished. The lengthy and celebrated political discussion between Mirabeau and the queen took place in the park, in 1790.

Under the Revolution the furniture was sold off and the château abandoned. But in 1799, while the régime of the Directoire was badly discredited, Sieyes began to spread rumors of a Jacobin plot. He arranged for the Conseils to be transferred to Saint-Cloud and for General Bonaparte to be appointed commander of the Paris troops. On May 18 1804, Napoleon, was proclaimed emperor at Saint-Cloud.

He commissioned Percier and Fontaine to restore the château; in 1810 he married Marie-Louise of Austria there. In 1815 the instrument of surrender to Blucher was signed in this same château. Then followed a brilliant period during which Charles V was in residence, under the ministry of Polignac. Saint-Cloud was where he decided on the disastrous decrees of 1830, which led to his downfall. And it was from there that he eventually fled, a defeated man.

Saint-Cloud was also the setting for Napoleon III's coronation as emperor of the French, and of his declaration of war on Prussia in July 1870. The château was burnt down during the siege of Paris, and for the next twenty-one years its charred hulk stood in stark remembrance of that terrible day. Eventually it was razed to the ground. The Ecole Normale Superieure for girls was built on the site of the outbuildings. Nowadays only the park and the waterfall remind us of the lavish splendor of Saint-Cloud in its prime.

was at Saint-Cloud that Napoleon was proclaimed Emperor of the French. Nothing remains now ut the park of the château, which attracts many sitors.

SCEAUX

The origin of the Sceaux estate can be traced back to Jehan Baillet, the treasurer of France during the reign of Louis XI, who owned a manor house on this site. At the end of the 16th century the lordship of Sceaux belonged to Louis Potier, *seigneur* of Gesvres and Tresmes, secretary of State under Henri III and Henri IV, who was descended from an illustrious Parisian family of magistrates. He divided his property among his three sons, giving the lordship of Sceaux to the youngest of them, Antoine, who then proceeded to rebuild the château in the Renaissance style. In 1674 the estate was acquired by Colbert, the famous minister of Louis XIV.

Jean-Baptiste Colbert was born into a very commonplace family of merchant drapers. After entering the service of Michel Le Tellier, secretary of state for war, he was introduced to Mazarin, who promptly discerned his merits and entrusted him with the management of his personal fortune.

who set up something approaching a full-scale court at the château, with brilliant guests such as Voltaire, Fontenelle and d'Alembert, Sceaux reached the height of its fame. The festivities known by the name 'Nuits de Sceaux' were long remembered. But the duchess allowed herself to be carried away by her penchant for intrigue, and became the ringleader of the celebrated but rather amateurish Célamare conspiracy, in which the ambassador of Spain plotted to overthrow the regent, Philippe d'Orleans. She had good reason to hate Philippe, but the plot was discovered and the duke went to jail.

In 1620, however, he was released and authorized to return to Sceaux. His sons, the prince de Dombes, and the comte d'Eu inherited the chateau; when they had died without issue their cousin, Louis de Bourbon, duc de Penthièvre, succeeded them. Due to his inspiration, it was not long before the château once again became a radiant center for French literary life. Florian, the author of fables, was his librarian.

Shortly before his death he recommended him to Louis XIV. The king was greatly impressed by the remarkable talents of Colbert, who uncovered for him the embezzlement committed by his financial supervisor Fouquet. Fouquet's fall from favor was followed by the meteoric rise of Colbert's political fortunes. In eight years he amassed titles and responsibilities and left his strong personal imprint on the reign of the Great King.

Notwithstanding his legendary sense of economy, he wanted a residence worthy of his standing in society. He had Claude Perrault, architect of the Paris Observatory and brother of the author of the famous fairy tales, renovate the old château of Gesvres, which had a highly classical appearance, with a central fore-part with lateral pavilions flanked by two wings on each side of a central courtyard. It was pleasantly decorated by Charles Le Brun, Coysvox and Tuby, while the gardens were obviously laid out by Le Nôtre. When Colbert died, his son, the marquis de Seignelay and minister of the navy, had Jules Hardouin-Mansart enlarge the garden, dig a Grand Canal and rebuild the Orangerie.

In 1700 Louis XIV decided to acquire the property for one of the sons he had by Madame de Montespan, the duc de Maine. As a result of the dynamism of the witty duchesse de Maine,

Curiously enough, the very popular duc de Pentièvre was not unduly disturbed during the Revolution; he died a natural death in 1793 — a most unusual occurrence for a former nobleman. However, as he had given the estate to his daughter, the duchesse d'Orleans, in 1791, her property was confiscated when she left France. Sceaux became home to a school of agriculture, and the property was sold in 1799 to a businessman from Saint Malo, Lecomte, who then took it into his head to demolish the chateau and loot the park. His son-in-law, the duc de Trevise and son of the *maréchal d'empire* Mortier, tried hard to repair the dreadful damage thus done by commissioning Lesoufache to build a brick chateau in a slightly bogus Louis XIII style, and replanted the park. When he died in 1902 the whole place was abandoned. The château, however, was bought in 1924 by the *département* of Seine, which restored it and, in 1937, inaugurated in it the museum of Ile de France.

The château of Sceaux houses the Museum of the Ile-de-France. Opposite: Several views of its very fine park.

PIERREFONDS

In the 11th century the lords of Pierrefonds—at name derived from mineral water springs knowns as *Petrae Fontes*—built a huge feudal castle at the edge of the forest of Compiègne. In 1392, when Louis d'Orleans, the brother of Charles VI, took possession of his Valois estates, he sought to protect them with a forbidding defensive network, and bought numerous more or less abandoned fortresses, among them Pierrefonds.

When fully restored, enlarged and richly renovated, the castle became not only a strategic fort but also a sumptuous Gothic residence. This pentagon, flanked by eight round towers, one of which was used as a chapel, was one of the most representative of all medieval structures. The towers and the façades had two superimposed walk ways, one of them with loopholes, the other with battlements. Niches contained statues of praying figures. An enormous square keep stands in the inner courtyard.

When Louis d'Orleans was assassinated by John the Fearless in 1407, the castle was already completed. It then passed to the charming poe Charles d'Orleans, who was to spend many years as a prisoner of the English. On his death in 1465 he bequeathed it to his son Louis, who became king of France in 1498. Early in the reign o

Henri IV the castle was taken by the members of the Catholic League, who were driven out of it in 1593. Somewhat later it was occupied by the group known as *Les Mécontents,* who were disappointed by the meeting of the Etats Generaux in 1614. Two years later it was besieged, captured and dismantled.

For nearly two and a half centuries Pierrefonds slumbered on, in ruins. But in 1857, Napoleon III decided to commission Viollet-le-Duc to restore it. This savior of so many historic monuments rebuilt it as an idealized medieval castle, just the way the Romantics might have imagined it. The external renovation was done quite faithfully, while much of the work on the inside was based on pure fantasy, although it owed much to Viollet-le-Duc's remarkable knowledge of Gothic architecture and feudal castles. His reconstruction has been greatly criticized, but it must be admitted that, were it not for this architect of genius, Pierrefonds would now be nothing more than a heap of uninteresting old stones.

The fortified castle of Pierrefonds bears the mark, both in its exterior — Cour d'Honneur (Courtyard of Honor) — and in its interior, of the Gothic style. It was magnificently restored by Viollet-le-Duc. Following pages: Two views of the château of Chantilly.

CHANTILLY

At the end of the 10th century the Le Bouteiller family, which included officers of the royal château of Senlis, built a powerful fortress in the midst of a small lake—the forerunner of a whole series of structures which were later to occupy the site. During the period of civil strife known as La Jacquerie, in 1358, it was destroyed. In 1386 Pierre d'Orgemont, who was first chancellor of the Dauphiné before becoming chancellor of France, acquired the estate and used the original materials to build a new fortress which closely follows the triangular shape of the islet.

In 1450 the heir to the Orgemont family fortunes, Marguerite, married the baron de Montmorency. In 1522 the chapel was restored by Guillaume, a descendant of that same illustrious family. He shared his property between his two sons, bequeathing to the eldest of them, Anne (a boy's name at the time), a companion of François I and a future constable, some large estates, including Chantilly.

Anne de Montmorency commissioned the architect Pierre I de Chambiges to modernize the château and to renovate the inner courtyard. Work was completed between 1527 and 1531, imparting to the Gothic superstructure a number of highly Italianate decorative features from the early Renaissance style. This type of architecture, not unlike that of some of the châteaux of the Loire and the Cour Ovale at Fontainebleau, was made known through a *Recueil d'Architecture* published by Androuet du Cerceau, though it was later amended to bring it into line with the second Renaissance period.

The royal hunting lodge known as the Petit Château, a handsome H-shaped building with balconies, consoles and mullioned windows, was built on another small island about this time.

Anne de Montmorency was killed fighting the Protestants at Saint-Denis in 1567. His eldest son François inherited Chantilly, which later went to the younger son Henri, who, like his father, became constable of France. Henri II, duc de Montmorency, the former's son, inherited the ancestral home in 1614. His wife, Maria Felice Orsini, who came from a very distinguished Italian family, was immortalized as the poetic heroine Sylvie, in the works of Theophile de Viau. The poet, who was suspected of atheism and persecuted by the Parliament, was housed by her in a small dwelling deep inside the park, known as La Maison de Sylvie.

After various episodes related to the upheavals of the period, Chantilly became the property of the great Condé family. It was Louis de Condé who routed the Spanish forces in a brilliant victory at Rocray. This military success, which

The château of Chantilly is situated on the bank of the Nonette, transformed into the Grand Canal of which a tributary passes through the French gardens. Opposite right: The Stag Gallery.

one branch, La Manche, flowed down the middle of a garden laid out in the French style.

Louis XIV was received in grand pomp at Chantilly on April 23 1671. Every conceivable effort was made to ensure that the state dinner would be a success. Unfortunately the promised delivery of fresh fish never materialized, and the *maître d'hotel,* in sheer despair, ran a sword through his body. As we learn from the marquise de Sévigné, such was the end of the famous Vatel, who had once worked under Fouquet.

As he grew older Condé tired of his château, finding it antiquated. He had it demolished and commissioned Jules Hardouin-Mansart to build him a new one. It was not a complete success. The building which rose from the old foundations was not always in harmony with the landscape. Condé, who was not known for his modesty, had Sauveur le Comte decorate the gallery known as the 'Gallery of the Prince's Prowess' with a series of paintings relating his military accomplishments. His death gave Bossuet an opportunity to deliver one of his most famous funerary orations, and Louis XIV said: "I have just lost the greatest man in my kingdom".

was merely the first of many, eventually won for him the nickname the 'Great Condé'. Later on he was one of the leaders of the aristocratic insurrection known as La Fronde des Princes, and, in an about-face which seems rather surprising to us today, he then fought on the Spanish side against France! When defeated by Turenne, he sought

and obtained clemency. Thereafter he made Chantilly his main residence.

Le Nôtre and La Quintinie laid out new gardens linked to the terrace by a monumental staircase, the Grand Degré, which Hardy decorated with two statues of Rivers. The local river, the Nonette, was turned into a Grand Canal, of which

His son and heir went ahead with construction, restored the Maison de Sylvie and built a menagery in the park. Work continued under the direction of Henri de Bourbon, the great-grandson of Le Grand Condé. Between 1719 and 1735 the architect Jean Aubert built the superb Grandes Ecuries (Great Stables), with room for one hundred and fifty horses, to the west of the château. This is certainly one of the most remarkable buildings of the entire 18th century, truly palatial in design, with its three pyramid-roofed pavilions, its gigantic arcades, its majestic pediment and its circular paddock, a truly spectacular sight.

The penultimate of the princes of Condé, Louis-Joseph, commissioned Leroy to build the long, sober and elegant residence known as the château d'Enghien, for his grandson, the duc d'Enghien. He also had English gardens laid out, with a cottage as required by the style of his day. After the storming of the Bastille this prince emigrated; in 1792 he set up a corps of guards which formed the nucleus of the future 'armée de Condé', which was to fight the Republic on the side of the Allies. When Louis-Joseph, at the age of seventy-eight, returned from exile with his son Louis-Henri-Joseph, who had also served in the counter-revolutionary armies, he found his estate broken down into fragments, the château razed to the ground and the furniture sold off. He recovered his property, and restored the Petit Château before his death in 1818. His descendant, the duc d'Aumale, had the Grand Château rebuilt on its foundations, between 1875 and 1882, in an imitation-Renaissance style. There is no denying that this new structure is better adapted to the site than its predecessor, designed by Mansart. The duke kept some fabulous collections of *objets d'art* and paintings at Chantilly, together with a considerable library. In 1897 he gave the estate and all its riches to the Institut de France.

The Chantilly gardens are linked to the terrace by a monumental staircase (top left) dominated by the statue of the "Great" Condé. The gardens were partly landscaped by Le Nôtre. Right: An annex of the château.

COMPIEGNE

Here we have another instance in which a passion for hunting, which seems to have been shared by most of the kings of France, led to the construction of one of the most remarkable royal abodes in Ile de France—the château de Compiègne. This place, which derives its name from that of an ancient Roman way-station, *Compendium*, meaning 'short-cut', is located in the midst of a huge forest well stocked with game. As early as the 6th century a Merovingian royal residence had been situated there. Charles II ('the Bald') built a castle—as well as an abbey—there and surrounded them with ramparts. The cylindrical 12th-century keep which stands gutted in a public garden of the town, may well have been the keep of a fortress dating from the time of the first Capetian kings. Yet the present château, which was built in the 18th century, was built on the site of another residence which had been erected by Charles V and later much altered and expanded over the centuries.

Louis XIV, who was a great hunter, stayed at Compiègne on seventy-five occasions, with much lavish entertaining; he did not, however, alter the medieval construction. On the other hand, Louis XV, who was also very fond of Compiègne, commissioned Jacques Gabriel to make some major renovations. The living quarters were then paneled, and the Tapestries of the Royal Hunt, produced by the Gobelins factory from cartoons by Oudry, which are still on display in one of the galleries of the new château, also date from this period. Jacques Gabriel died in 1742 and was succeeded by his son Jacques-Ange. It was he who designed the Place Louis XV (now Place de la Concorde) and the Ecole Militaire. He was commissioned by Louis XV to build a new and much bigger château on the site of the old.

The new royal abode extends over more than five acres, in a highly academic and thus rather cold style. Its triangular shape was dictated by shortage of space. The extent to which the château could be enlarged was limited by the expansion of the town itself, and it was thus

necessary to build on the old foundations. The main facade, for example, is curiously situated at an oblique angle to the main courtyard. That garden façade is 960 ft. long. On the second side the large square courtyard is separated from the place du Palais, in front of the château, by a majestic double colonnade. The buildings are three storeys high and there are three projecting sections decorated with pilasters and Doric columns. The roofs are often hidden, in the Italian manner, by a balustrade. Two majestic staircases ascend to the main floor, where the royal apartments are located.

In this same château, in 1770, the Dauphin, paralyzed by shyness, received Marie-Antoinette, archduchess of Austria, several days before their wedding at Versailles. In 1785 the royal apartment and the south wing were at last completed. A terrace was laid out on the side of the park. But the queen, who busied herself with decoration and furnishing, never found the time to live there, on account of the Revolution. Despite all the turmoil of the times, the château was fortunately left

intact, although the furniture was removed.

Napoleon was very fond of Compiègne. While he was in power the architect Berthault renovated the interior, with the result that in many instances adjacent sections of the decor are found to consist of the styles of the Louis XVI period and magnificent samples of the style of the Empire. It is worth noting that it was also at Compiègne that the emperor, on March 29 1810, received his future and second wife, Marie-Louise—also arch-duchess of Austria—and niece of Marie-Antoi-nette! It was raining heavily at the time, but the ardor of Napoleon's welcome for her was undimi-nished.

The most remarkable rooms in the imperial apartments are the Salon des Fleurs, its walls lined with mirrors and with piers painted by Redouté and Dubois, the library, the bedroom of Marie-Louise and the Salon Bleu. Most of the furniture was designed by Jacob. Between two secondary countyards Percier and Fontaine built the Ballroom, surrounded by a huge colonnade.

Soon after coming to power in 1832, Louis-Philippe celebrated the third princely wedding in the history of the château—that of his daughter Louise and Leopold I, first king of the Belgians. They were united in the chapel, the decor of which dates from the same period.

Yet the heyday of Compiègne was to come with Napoleon III and his wife Empress Eugénie, who assembled a brilliant court and did some sump-tuous entertaining. Guests were often invited according to a special kind of serial system, grouping together eighty people of a particular social or professional category. The receptions would last ten days. Bedrooms were in short supply, and some guests, despite their elevated rank, had to sleep in the attic. Compiègne was the scene of much dancing, hunting, comedy and general merrymaking. One rainy day, in order to keep the guests entertained, Mérimée recited his famous 'Dictation': the empress beat the record for the number of mistakes, with a total of eighty-three.

She was in charge of the choice of new furniture. She adored the 18th century, but some-times had to be content with copies. The château also contained furniture characteristic of the Second Empire style—rich but heavy. The events of 1870 interrupted the construction of a new theater, which had been made necessary by the

size of women's crinoline skirts. The number of seats available had to be cut from 800 to 600!

Under the Third Republic, in 1901, President Loubet was host to Tsar Nicolas II. Nowadays the château houses several museums, including one dealing with the Second Empire which contains Winterhalter's masterpiece *Empress Eugénie sur-rounded by her ladies at the palace.* One of the minor courtyards has been covered over to protect the collections of the Automobile Museum. Every effort has been made, in most of the rooms of the château, to make use of inventories from the period so as to ensure that both furniture and decor accurately reflect those of the various periods during the history of Compiègne.

It is to Napoleon III and the Empress Eugénie that Compiègne owes its hour of glory. Top: Two views of the château; Opposite: A detail of the façade; bottom: La Cour d'Honneur (Courtyard of Honor) and la Galerie de Bal (The Ball Gallery).

RARAY

There was a fortress on this site as early as the 13th century, but the present château dates from the beginning of the 17th century, when Nicolas de Lancy built a rectangular structure flanked by two pavilions. During the reign of Louis XV the marquis des Barres drastically altered the architectural unity of the place by adding an attic to the central building and semicircular pediments to the pavilions. The roofs were fringed with balustrades, and bull's-eyes and garlands were added, in keeping with the taste of the times.

But the really distinctive trait of Raray is the work of Nicolas de Lancy : the main courtyard, in which each of the side walls has a central door and eighteen arcades separated by niches containing busts in the ancient manner. Two hunting scenes—one involving deer and the other wild boar—stand out in rounded low relief along the entablature. Since the Renaissance hunting has inspired many a decor, but such a presentation is surely rare. It is done in a typically Baroque taste and in the Italian style.

An isolated monumental gateway in the middle of the park is decorated with cariatids, with the sculpted allegory of the Lady with the Unicorn along its pediment. Much more recently the main courtyard of Raray was the setting in which Jean Cocteau's film *Beauty and the Beast* was shot.

The exterior of the château of Raray bears the characteristics of both the medieval period and the style of the XVIIth century. Right: La Cour d'Honneur (Courtyard of Honor) decorated with remarkable motifs depicting a stag hunt (baroque style).

ANET

The famous architect and engraver Androuet du Cerceau has left us a superb drawing of the château of Diane de Poitiers which conveys a very good idea of the vast harmony of its buildings, arranged around three contiguous courtyards and a broad fortified quadrangle.

Diane was the daughter of Jean de Poitiers, comte de Saint-Vallier. Around 1515 she married Louis de Brézé, a friend of the family who was very much her senior, and became one of the queen's ladies-in-waiting. She was stunningly beautiful. In 1523 her father, found guilty of taking part in the conspiracy of Constable de Bourbon, was sentenced to death. Diane begged François I to spare him. What did she promise him in exchange? There was a great deal of speculation on the subject, but no hard facts. It was not until the very last moment, on the scaffold, that the count learned that he had been pardoned.

Diane became a widow in 1531 and inherited the château d'Anet. For the rest of her lige she wore black and white as a sign of mourning, though she might also have done so out of coquettishness. At any rate, the timid Dauphin the future Henri II, who was married to Catherine de Médicis, was so taken with her that she became his mistress towards 1536—apparently with the blessing of François I. Once her lover had become king, she found herself in a virtually sovereign position. Now she was more haughty than ever supremely elegant and increasingly beautiful. She certainly reigned supreme over art and literature Henri gave her Chenonceau, but she spent mos of her time at Anet, which she turned into a sumptuous residence.

She chose Philibert Delorme as her architect and work began in 1548. All the great artists of her day—Jean Goujon, Germain Pilon, Benvenute Cellini and Léonard Limousin, the great enamele —contributed to the decor. While respecting th old building erected by the Brézé family in th 15th century, Delorme completely covered it over

The main courtyard was closed to form a façade by the addition of three doors inlaid with marble in the form of a triumphal arch. The chapel, the Orangerie, the outbuildings and the arcaded galleries make a harmonious whole. The pilasters, columns and painted ceilings and panels constitute a triumph of Italian art. One is constantly reminded of the name of the lady who owned the house by a multitude of allusions to Diana, the hunting goddess of mythology.

Diane's royal lover—twenty years her junior—was still captivated by her beauty when he was accidentally killed during a tournament by the comte de Montgomery. Diane immediately found herself out in the cold: Catherine de Médicis took Chenonceau back from her—giving her in exchange the rather somber Chaumont—and sent her packing to her estate. Until her death in 1566 she lived mainly at Anet, which she continued to embellish. In keeping with her wishes, her daughter Louise, duchesse d'Aumale, had a funerary chapel built in her memory outside the château limits.

Under Louis XIII Anet became the property of the adulterine son of Henri IV, César de Vendôme, whose grandson Joseph, duc de Vendôme, altered the château by rebuilding the façade in the classical style.

The château of Anet, where Italian art dominates, is a masterpiece of harmony. Left: The Red Salon and the Dining-Hall. Right: Diane de Poitiers' bed and the paving of the Royal Chapel. Following pages: The Main Staircase at Anet.

MAINTENON

The first lords of this piece of land were vassals of the comte de Montfort. Their 13th-century fortress took the form of a quadrangle strengthened at the corners by a stout square stone keep and three round brick towers. In 1505 Louis XII's financial treasurer, Jean Cottereau, bought the property. He retained the keep and the towers, but built on two sides of the quadrangle a main residential section and an L-shaped wing. The other two sides remained as fortified outer walls. In 1526 Jean Cottereau's daughter married Jacques Angennes, lord of Rambouillet, and the estate became the property of the family until the 17th century, when it was bought by the marquis de Villeray. The central building was still a rather gloomy piece of architecture, but it was soon to change, in the hands of the woman who was to bear its name.

Françoise d'Aubigné was the grand-daughter of Agrippa d'Aubigné, one of the Protestant leaders during the wars of religion, a companion of Henri IV and the author of a remarkable poem, *Les Tragiques*. After being born in prison at Niort, where her parents were being detained for high treason, she spent part of her youth in Martinique, coming to Paris after her father's death in 1645. She then renounced Protestantism, probably more out of necessity than conviction; in order to escape from poverty, in 1652, she married the poet Scarron, a paralytic, ugly and quite elderly gentleman, endowed, however, with

The château of Maintenon: The park, the entrance of the Cour d'Honneur (Courtyard of Honor) and the aqueduct. Françoise d'Aubigné received the estate from Louis XIV in 1674.

considerable wit, and her salon was quite famous.

When she was widowed in 1660 she managed to stay 'virtuous'—a remarkable fact much commented on at the time—despite her great poverty and outstanding beauty. In 1669 she was appointed governess to the adulterine children of Louis XIV and Madame de Montespan. Her friendship with the king dates from this period. Montespan's influence began to decline, until, shortly after the 'Affaire des Poisons', she was sent into exile.

The king was increasingly impressed by the wisdom and the restraint of Françoise. In 1674 he offered her the château of Maintenon; in 1680 he appointed her lady-in-waiting to the Dauphine; and in 1684, after the death of his wife, he married her, secretly and morganatically. During the closing years of the reign she imposed on the court at Versailles an austerity which bordered on bigotry. The former Protestant proved to be a severe Catholic.

As soon as she took possession of the Maintenon estate, Françoise d'Aubigné undertook a complete renovation. Opposite the wing built by Jean Cottereau she built another wing, thus sealing off the main courtyard. Here she arranged her private residence, which included a huge antechamber draped with embossed and gilded leather. The outer wall which made up the fourth side of the original quadrangle was demolished, thus opening up a clear view of a park designed by Le Nôtre, as far as the arches of the aqueduct which was to bring the waters of the Eure to Versailles.

The château of Maintenon. Opposite left: The Small and Large Salons. Right: The Duchess of Adryen's sedan chair and the Cenotaph in memory of Madame de Maintenon. Below: A door in the turret ornamented by an effigy of St. Michael overcoming the dragon.

VINCENNES

The forest of Vilcena was mentioned as far back as the 9th century in ancient chronicles. The area abounded with deer, boar and other game; and for that very reason, three hundred years later, Louis VII ('the Young') built a hunting lodge there. This was replaced by a castle under Philippe-Auguste. Saint-Louis built another on the same site as well as a chapel to house a fragment of the crown of thorns which had been brought back from Jerusalem. The memory of this king still hovers over Vincennes through his chronicler Joinville, who portrays him administering justice seated under an oak.

Vincennes castle continued to be one of the preferred residences of the direct Capetians. Joan of Navarre, wife of Philip the Fair, and two of her sons, Louis X le Hutin and Charles IV ("the Fair") all died there. It may well have been here also that Jean the Posthumous, the son of Louis X and Clemence of Hungary, was poisoned at his baptism.

Upon the death of the last direct Capetian, Philippe VI de Valois acceded to the throne. He began the construction of the present keep in 1337. This splendid sample of the civil architecture of the Middle Ages was continued by Jean II ('the Good') and completed by Charles V, who had been born at Vincennes and who preferred it as a residence to any other. He built the nearby château of Beauté, which his grandson Charles VIII presented as a girl to his mistress Agnès Sorel, who became known thereafter as the 'Dame de Beauté'. In the king's view of things, Vincennes was to be a fortified town with the huge keep dominating the scene. That is why, around 1375, he built a huge rectangular defensive wall some 4,000 feet long flanked by nine square towers; within this vast inner courtyard near the manor of Saint-Louis, he built a new Sainte-Chapelle, the nave of which is a model of elegance.

However, even at the time of their construction, these fortifications, were already out of date; as a result, Vincennes was to remain more of a residence than of fortress. Charles VI lived there. When he went mad his wife Isabeau de Bavière, acting as regent, signed with the English the Treaty of Troyes, which placed the kingdom in foreign hands. In this way, in 1420, Vincennes came under the control of Henry V of England, who had been proclaimed king of France. He died two years later. In 1436, however, the castle was taken by Jacques de Chabannes, lord of La Palice, who returned it to Charles VII, who was all the more delighted to have it as his residence since Agnès Sorel lived nearby.

Louis XI resided fairly often at Vincennes. He abandoned the keep and built a more modern dwelling, backing onto the south part of the west wall. The keep then became a State prison, under the control of Olivier le Daim, known also as Olivier le Diable ('devil'), a famous barber and counsellor to the king; it retained this status until 1784.

Vincennes was where François I received the ambassadors of Suleiman the Magnificent and negotiated the Ottoman Alliance. Under Henri II, Philibert Delorme completed the Sainte-Chapelle, while respecting its Gothic style. The stained glass windows are the work of master glassmaker Beaurain. The last of the Valois often went to Vincennes, and Charles IX died there in 1574. It was also the setting, in 1587, for the marriage

The château of Vincennes seen from the air Above: The south angle.

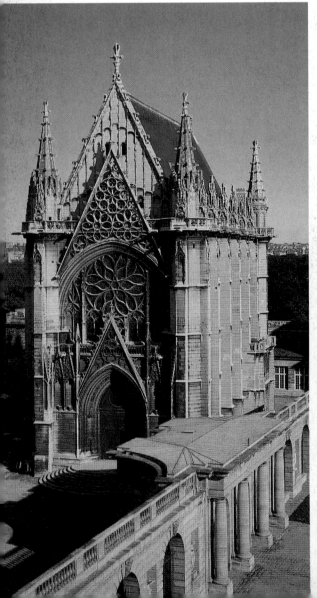

(arranged by Henri III) between one of the king's favorite minions, the duc d'Epernon, and Marguerite de Foix-Candale, in the midst of lavish and at times rather saucy festivities.

After his father's death, Louis XIII built a new royal abode, bigger than that of Louis XI. During his reign the keep served as a prison for Henri II de Bourbon-Condé, the maréchal d'Ornano, Alexandre and César de Vendôme. Later, during the Fronde, the duc de Beaufort, the Grand Condé, the prince de Conti, the duc de Longueville and cardinal de Retz were all held in custody there.

It was under Mazarin that Louis Le Vau and François d'Orbay built the handsome classical structures which surround Louis XIII's building. After a brief stay Louis XIV left Vincennes for Versailles. The keep's sole occupants at the time were a number of distinguished prisoners : Fouquet, Voisin, famous for her skill with poisons, and then in the 18th century, Diderot and Mirabeau.

In 1804, Bonaparte had the young duc d'Enghien shot in the ditches at Vincennes. During the Empire the château was turned into an arsenal and in 1814 as in 1815 its governor, General Daumesnil, put up a heroic resistance to the Allies. The architecture suffered as a result. In the 19th century Saint-Louis' old manor house was demolished, the towers were razed and the ditches were filled in. In 1944 the Wehrmacht blew up part of the king's pavilion. Large-scale restoration work is now in progress.

The château of Vincennes bears the marks of very different periods, as can be seen from these views. Left: The Gothic chapel. Right: The donjon.

GROSBOIS

The château of Grosbois was built around 1580 by Raoul Moreau, treasurer of savings under the reign of Henri III. After his death, his son-in-law sold it to Charles de Valois, the adulterine son of Charles IX and Marie Touchet, who was to give the building its current appearance. The four corner pavilions and the two wings with arcaded galleries on the ground floor around the main courtyard date from 1615-1620.

Grosbois has one original feature which was to be found later at Versailles: the open courtyard leads, over successive levels, to the main façade like a semicircle crowned by a triangular pediment. A complex pattern of slate roofs lends great variety to the structure.

Its owners have included Germain Louis de Chauvelin, a confident of cardinal Fleury, and the comte de Provence, who later became Louis XVIII. Curiously enough, the Revolution spared Grosbois, which somehow managed to flourish at the same time. In 1797 Barras, a former member of the Convention, a regicide, one of those who eliminated Robespierre, bought the property once he had become a member of the Directoire. He retired to it after the 18 Brumaire. In 1804 Marshal Berthier bought it; he had the great gallery decorated with the busts of the other marshals of the Empire and scenes from his battles. The Pompeian decor of his bedroom is still a fine sample of the style of the period. Recently his descendants have sold the château to a horse-breeding institution.

Above: The château of Grosbois with its slate roofs. Its original character made it a forerunner of Versailles.

COURANCES

This château in the Louis XIII style stands to the west of the forest of Fontainebleau. The original structure, built by Cosme Clause, secretary of state under Henri II and lord of Fleury-en-Bière around 1550, was quite different. The present château, which was renovated about 1622 by Claude Gallard, counsellor to the king, consists of a plain rectangular building flanked by pavilions with independent roofs. The materials used were brick and stone — the latter forming tiles. The lower floor was intended for the staff, while the reception and residential rooms, on two floors, are illuminated through large rectangular bay windows.

In the 19th century two external staircases — imitating the Horseshoe at Fontainebleau — and a new wing were added. A majestic tree-lined avenue leads to the wrought-iron grill which closes off the forecourt, a broad grassy esplanade flanked by two canals. The château, which is surrounded by moats, is in the superb setting of a park designed by Le Nôtre in which ponds and canals stretch all the way down to the regulated waters of the River Ecole.

There is a curious Japanese garden on the left of the park. Inside, a marble salon in the style of Louis XIV, and several reception rooms with magnificent Louis XV wood paneling, are still in excellent condition.

The château of Courances is characterised by its soberness. Its park laid out by Le Nôtre is brightened by ornamental pools and canals. Last page: the château of Champs, a fine symbol of the noble dwellings of the Ile-de-France.